A LOOK INTO

American Indian art
Pre-Columbian Art

Conceived, Designed, and Illustrated by:

Mrinal Mitra

Series edited by:

Swarna Mitra & **Malika Mitra**

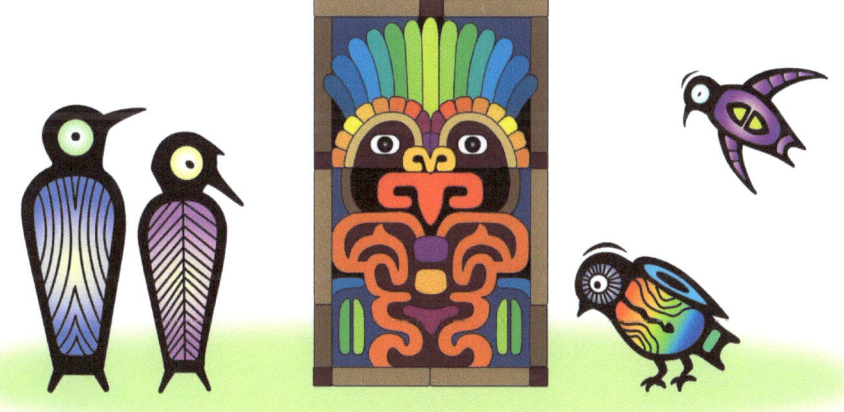

This series is dedicated to the citizens of the world;
from the young blooming minds of children, to the aspired individuals of all ages.

THE WORLD CULTURE ART
VOLUME-2

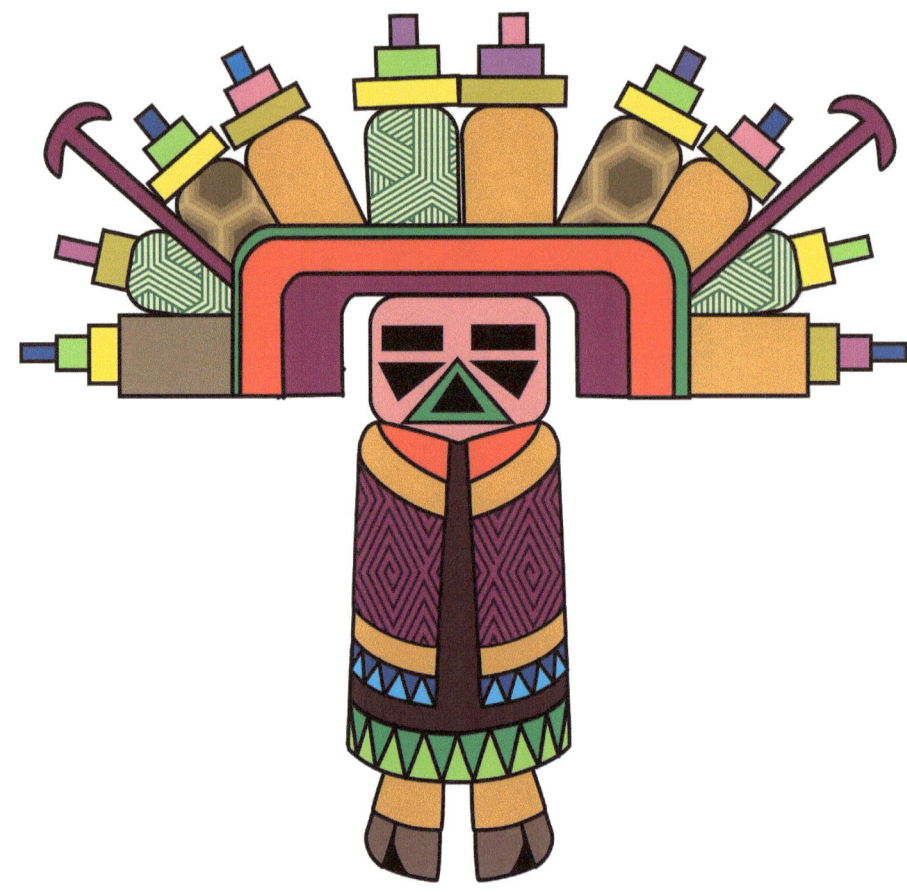

Salako Kachina, carved by Arizona Hopisin about 1900.

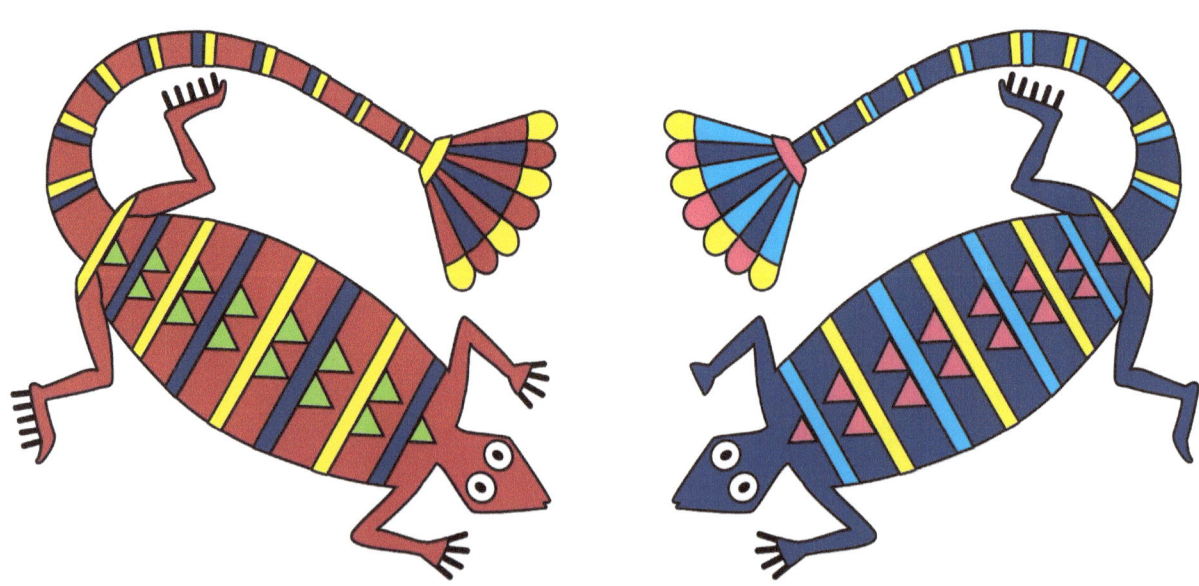

Mimbres figurative elements with geometric designs on the jar. New Mexico, USA, 1981.

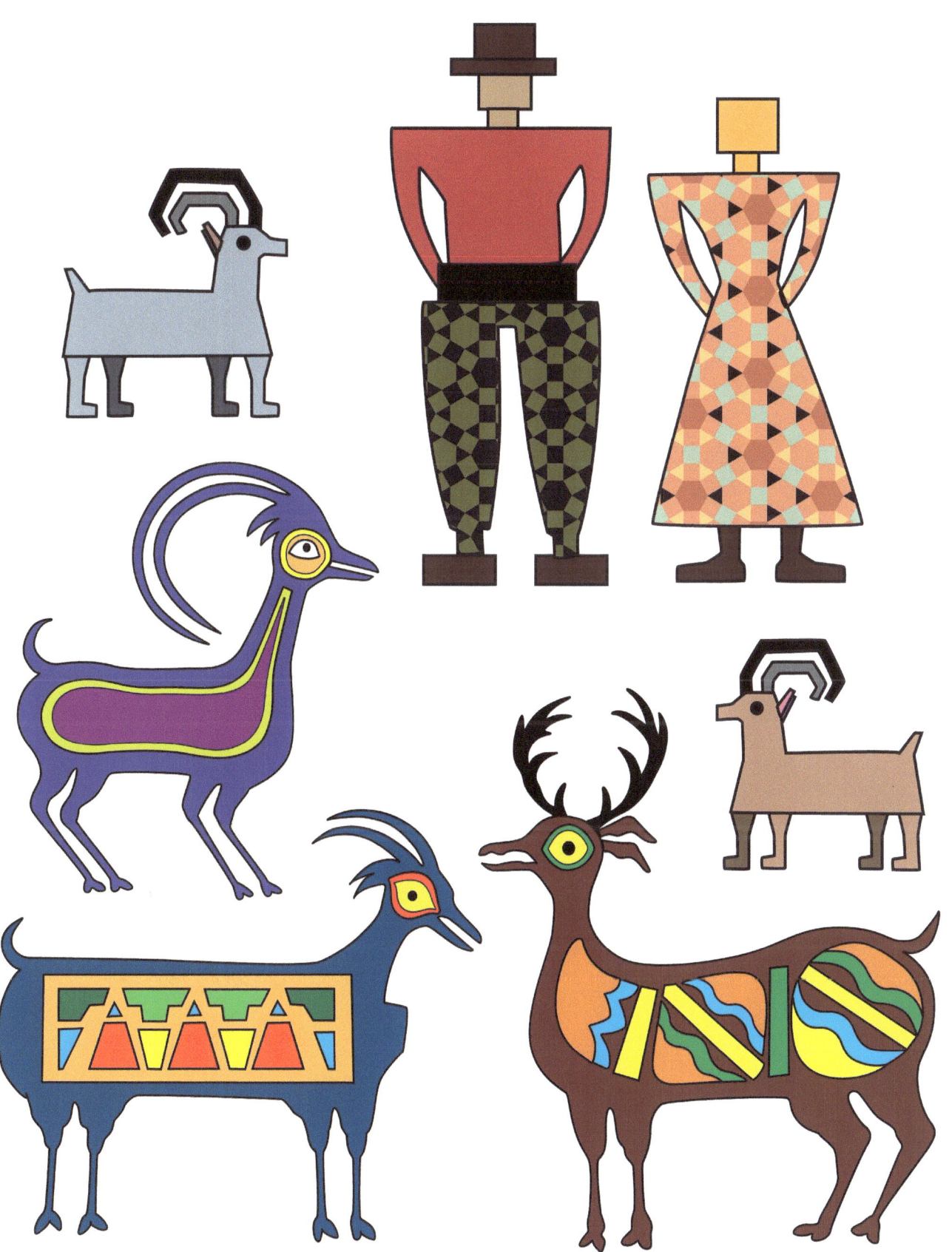

Highly stylized human beings and animals from Pueblo potters,
Southwestern America, (Arizona and New Mexico, USA).

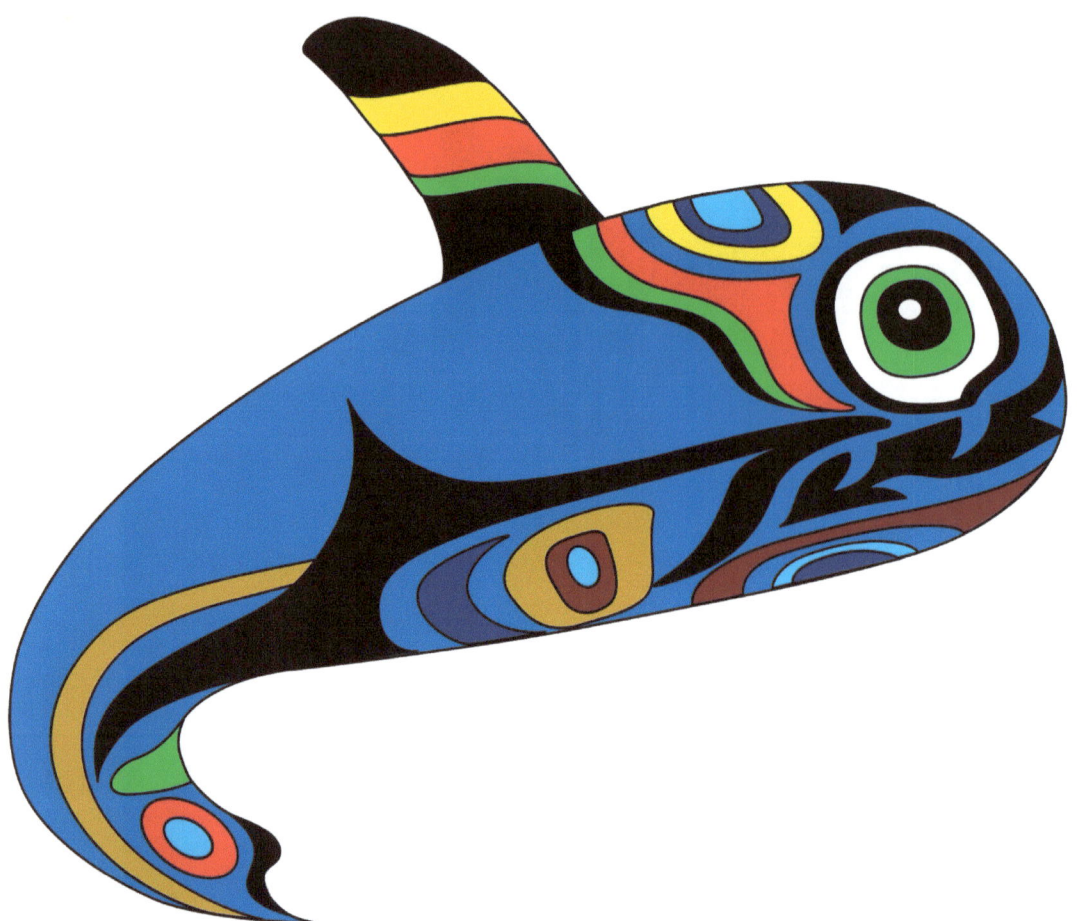

Stylized Killer Whale on a decorated pole. Vancouver Island, Canada.

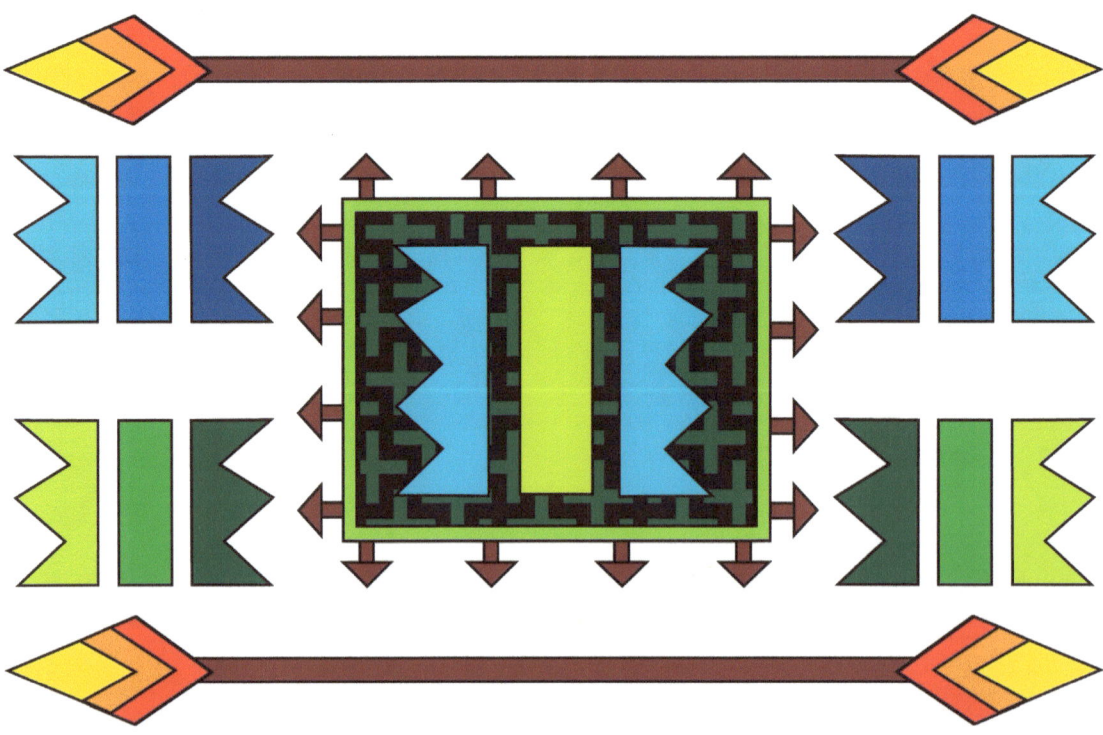

Bold geometric designs on corn-husk bag by Nez Perce artist 1920.

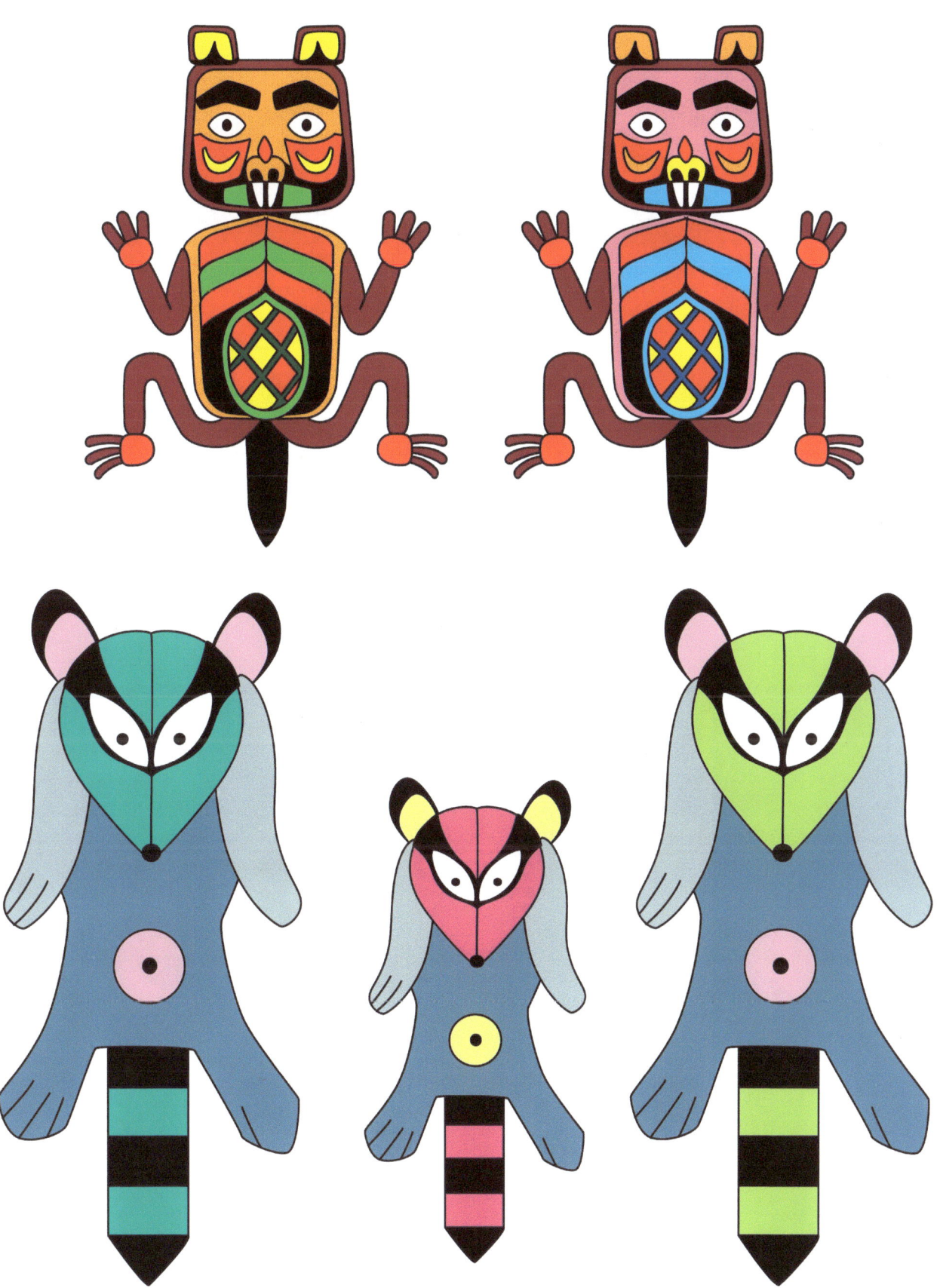

Images of raccoons and a beavers on a button blanket. Northwest Coast.

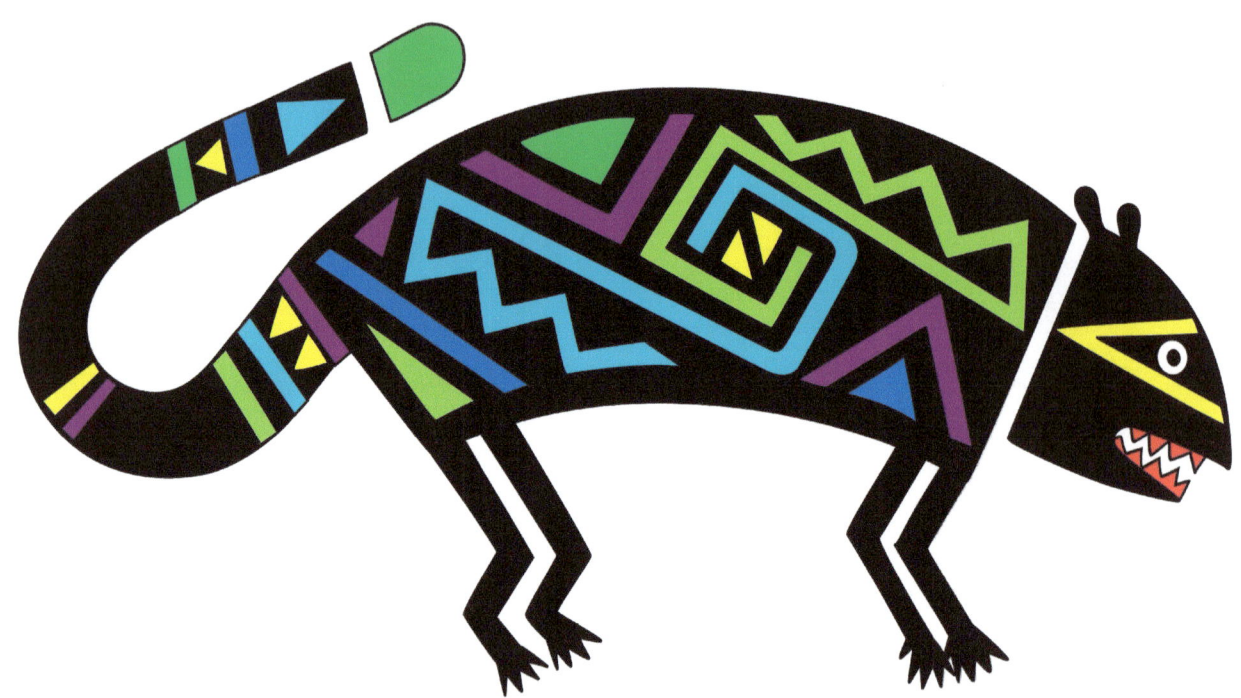

Stylized animal. Pueblo pottery. Southwestern USA.

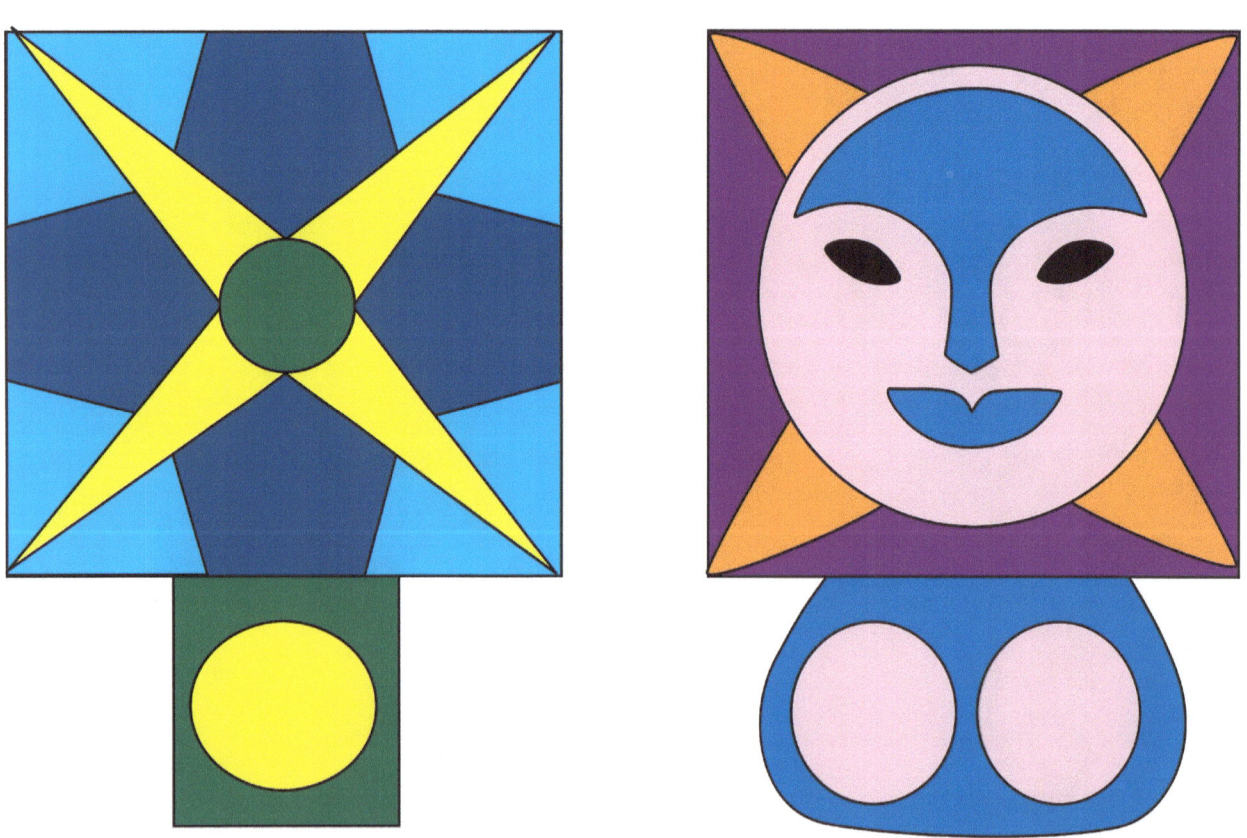

Finger Masks created by the Eskimos of North America.

American Indian Art

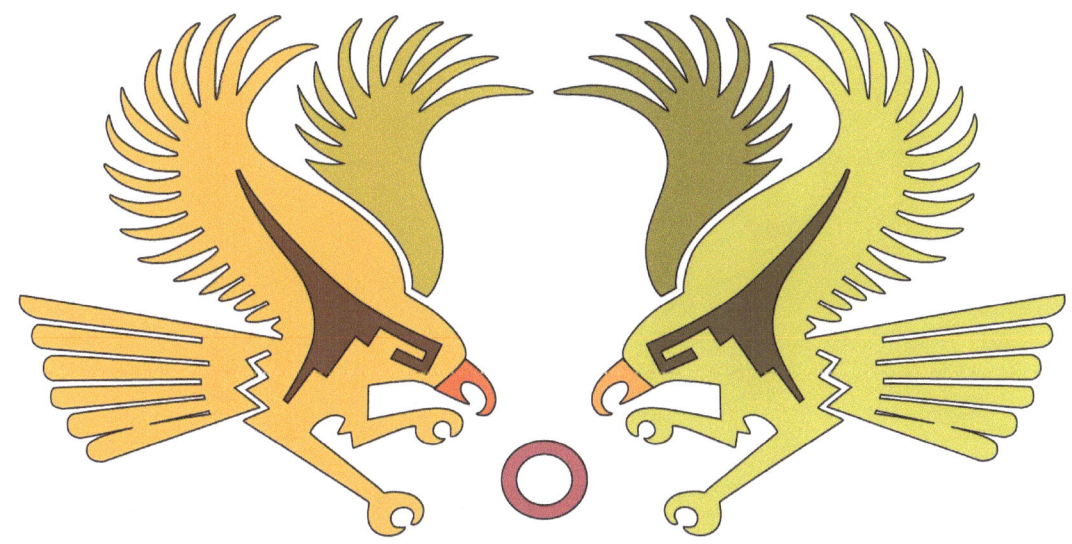

Objects of extraordinary beauty was produced by Hopi jewelers.
Hopis lived in Arizona and New Mexico, USA.

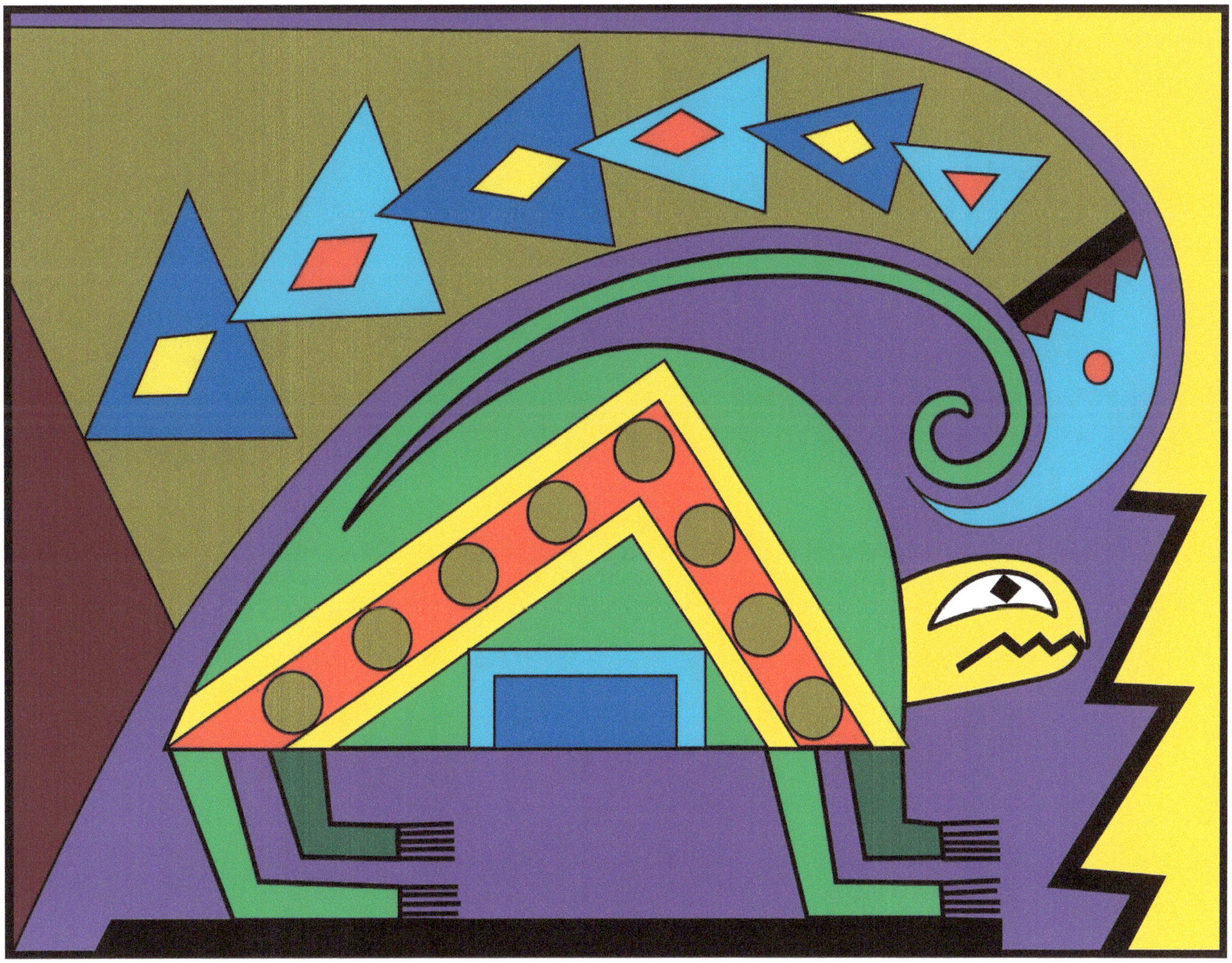

From an American Native painting. The painter explores ancient beliefs and anthropomorphized forces
of nature as depicted in Hopi, Navajo, and ancient Mimbres cultures.

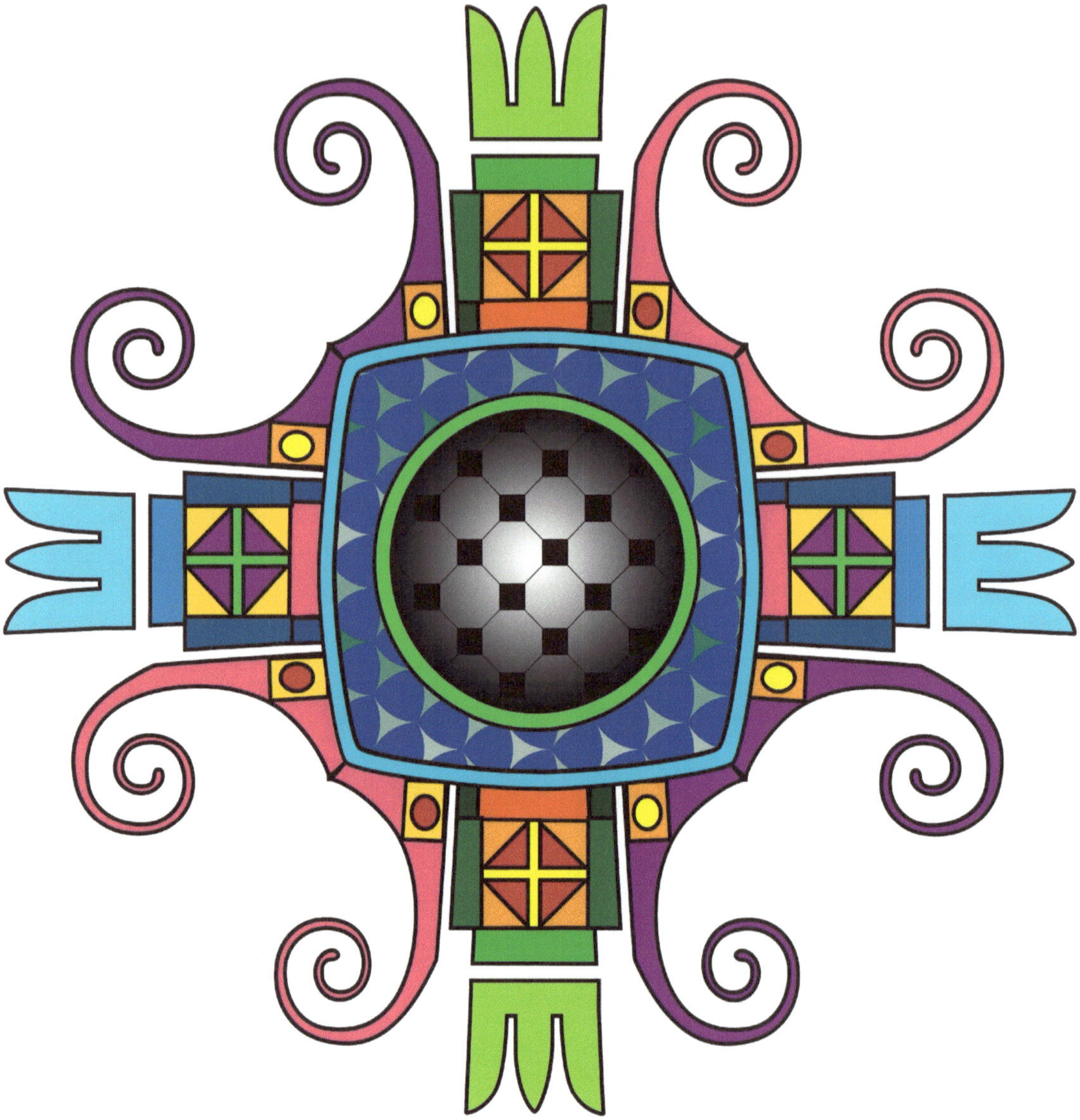

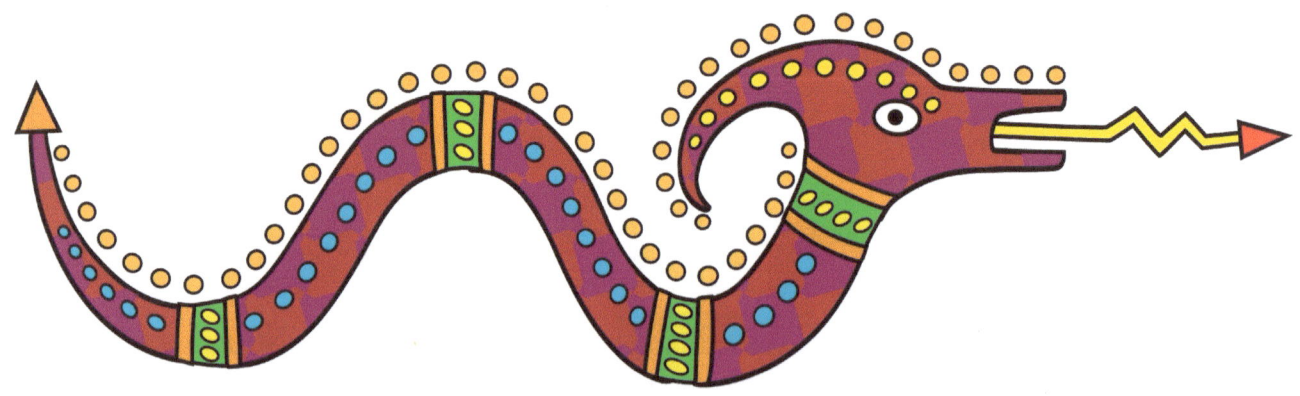

Design on jar created by Nampeyo, the famed Hopi potter. Early 20th Century.

Lightning Snake- The Northwest Coast art.

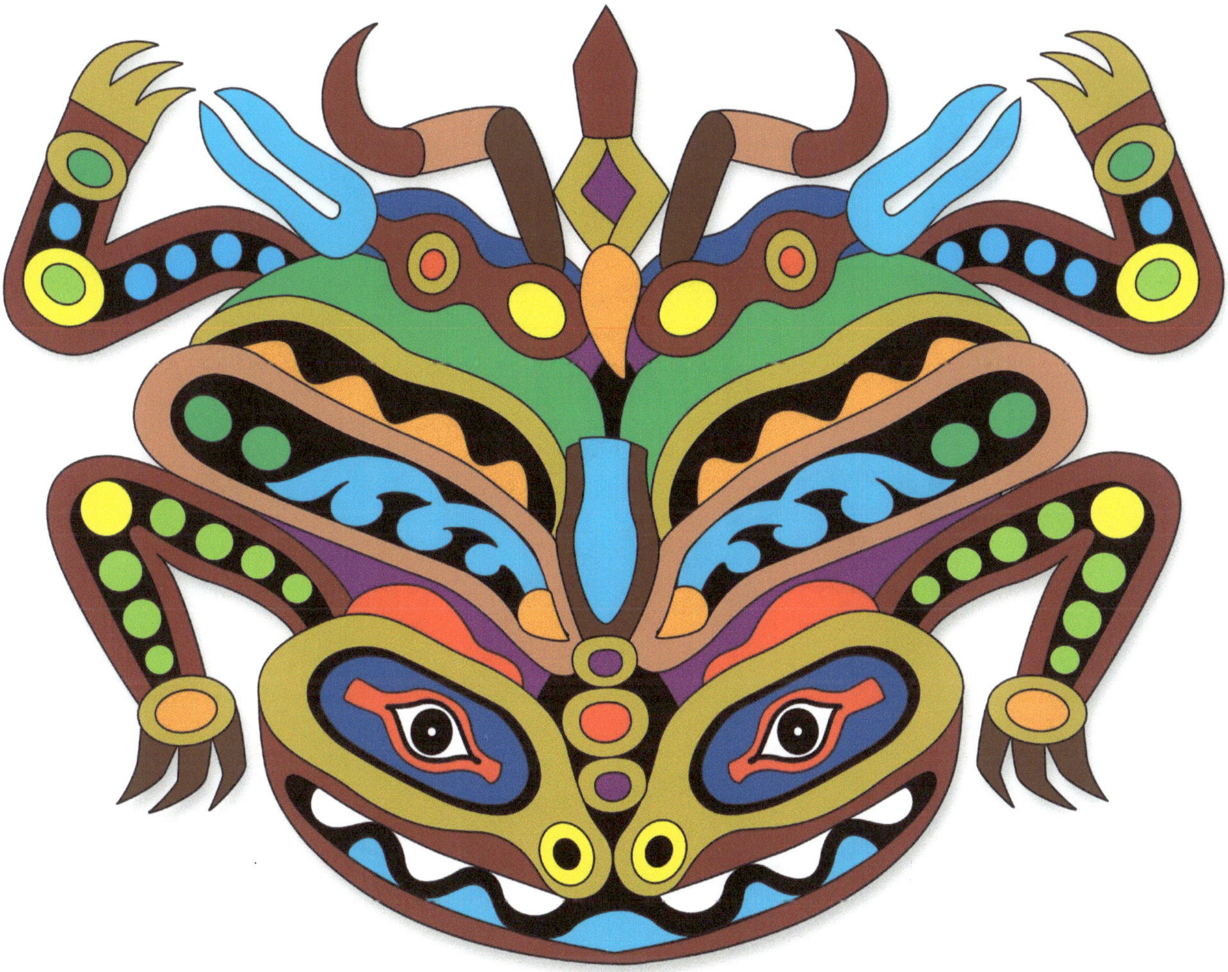

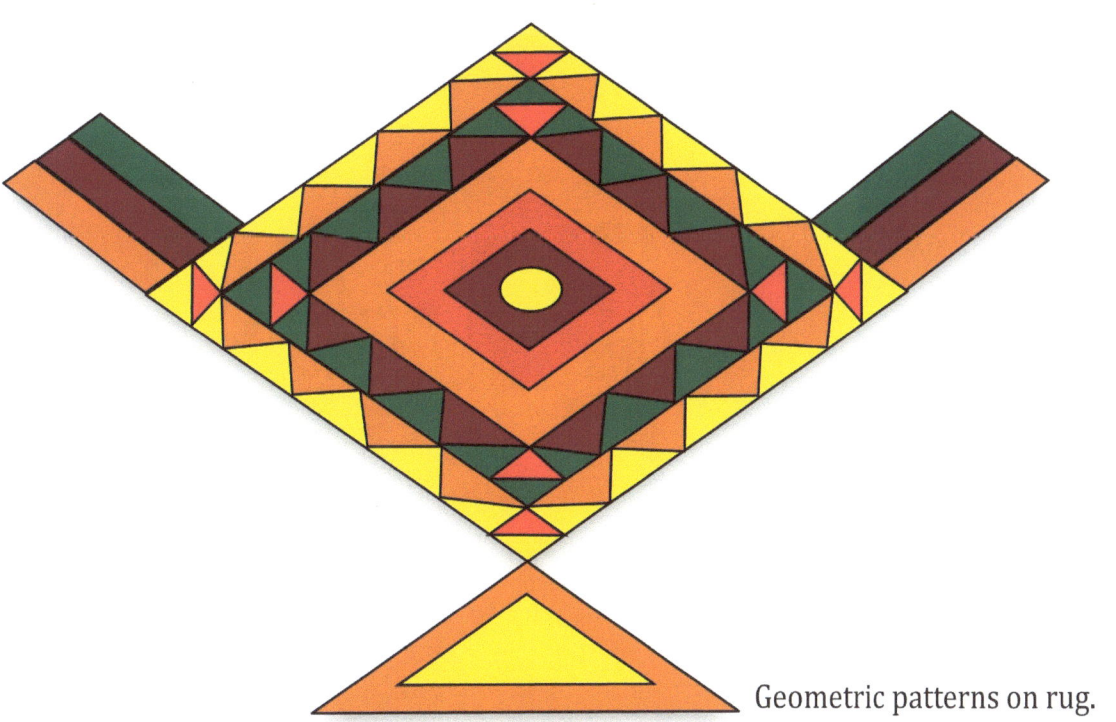

Frog on leggings, illustrating the flamboyant quality of the style. Tlingit, 1880 C.E.

Geometric patterns on rug.

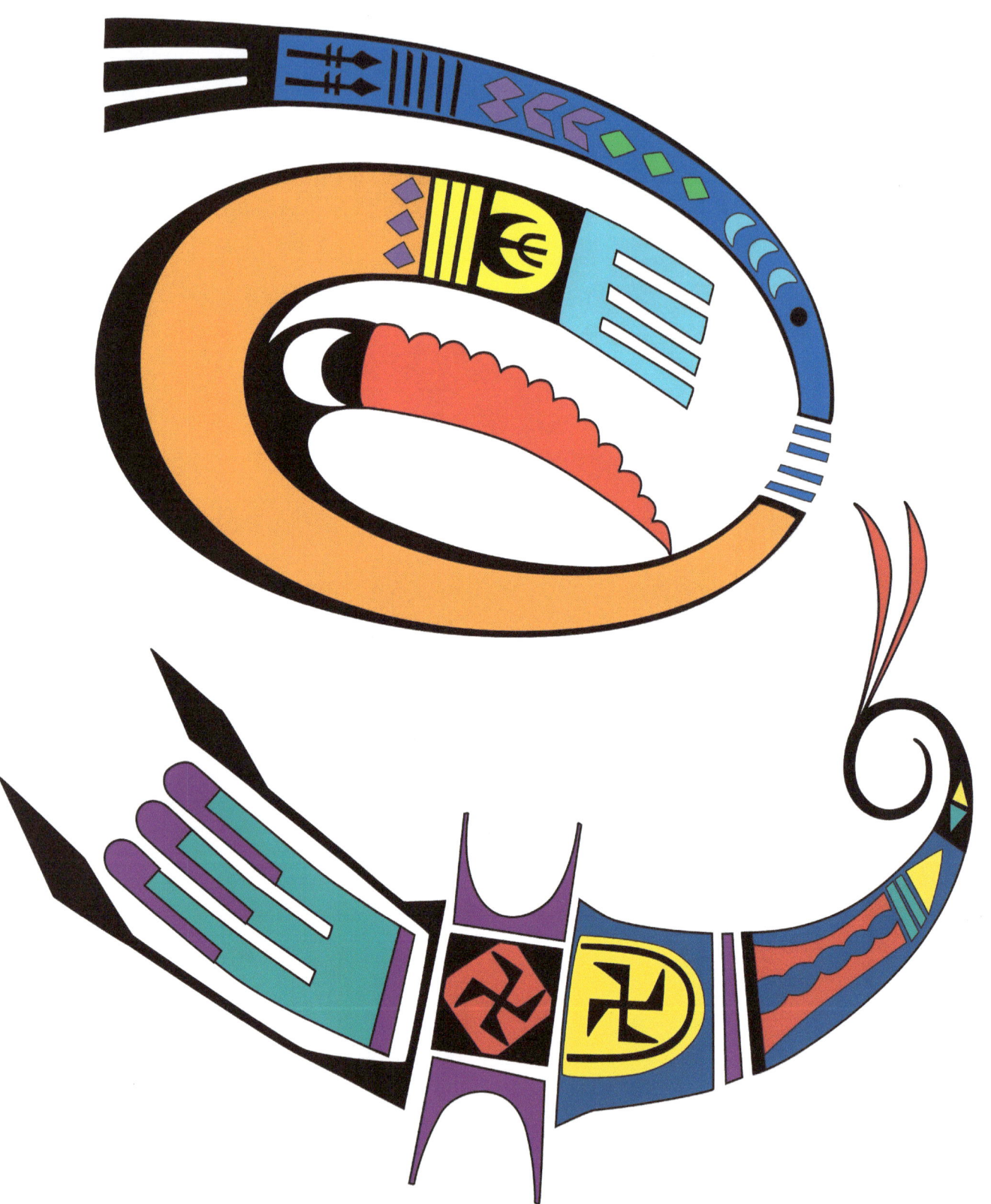

The famed Hopi potter Nampeyo adopted prehistoric motifs
in the 20th Century. These images are
abstracted body parts and feathers of birds, Southwest USA.

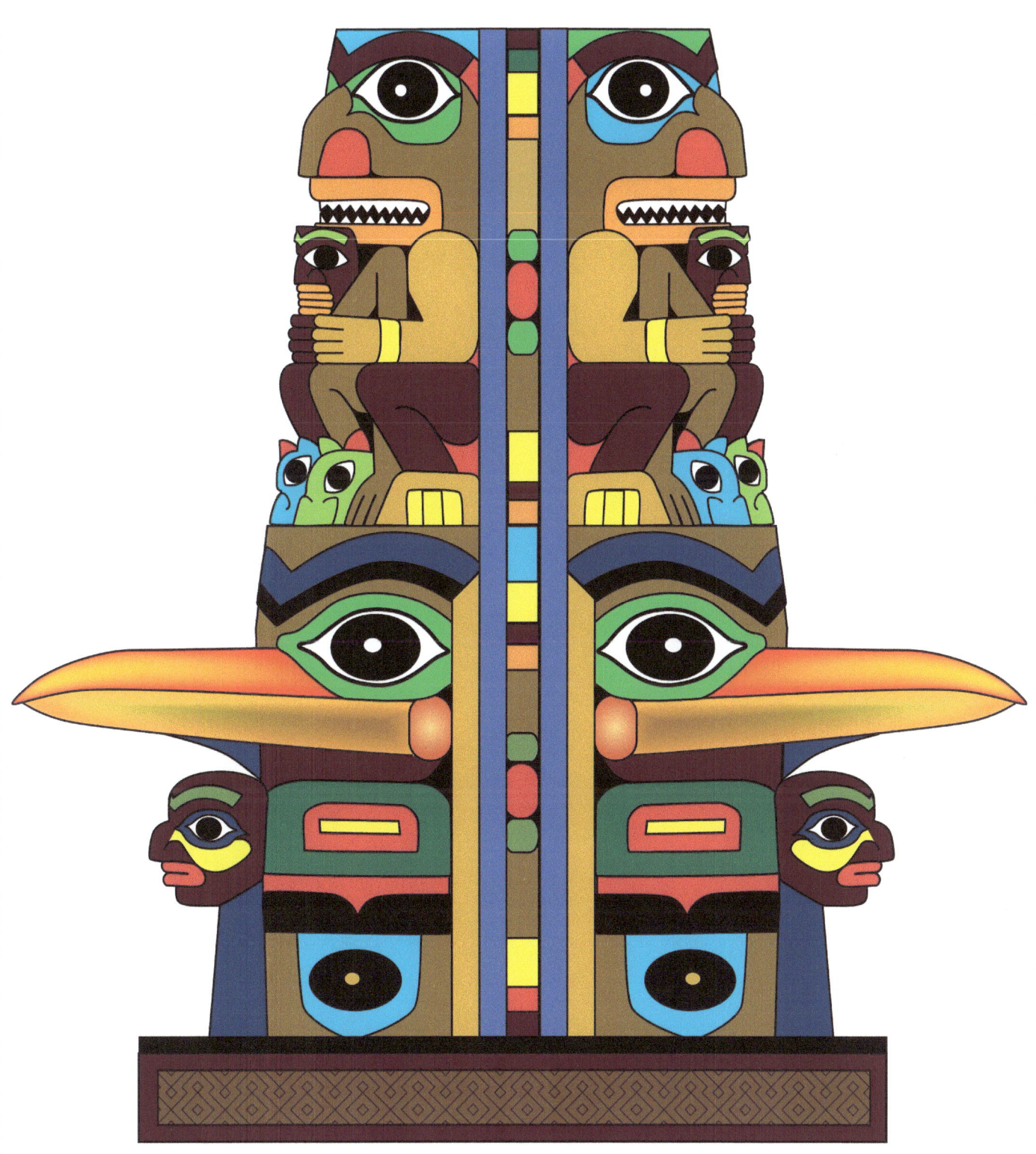

Part of a Haida Heraldic or Totem Pole.
When a person of dignitary dies, his successor or
other members of his family would raise
a pole in his honor. Vancouver Island, Canada.

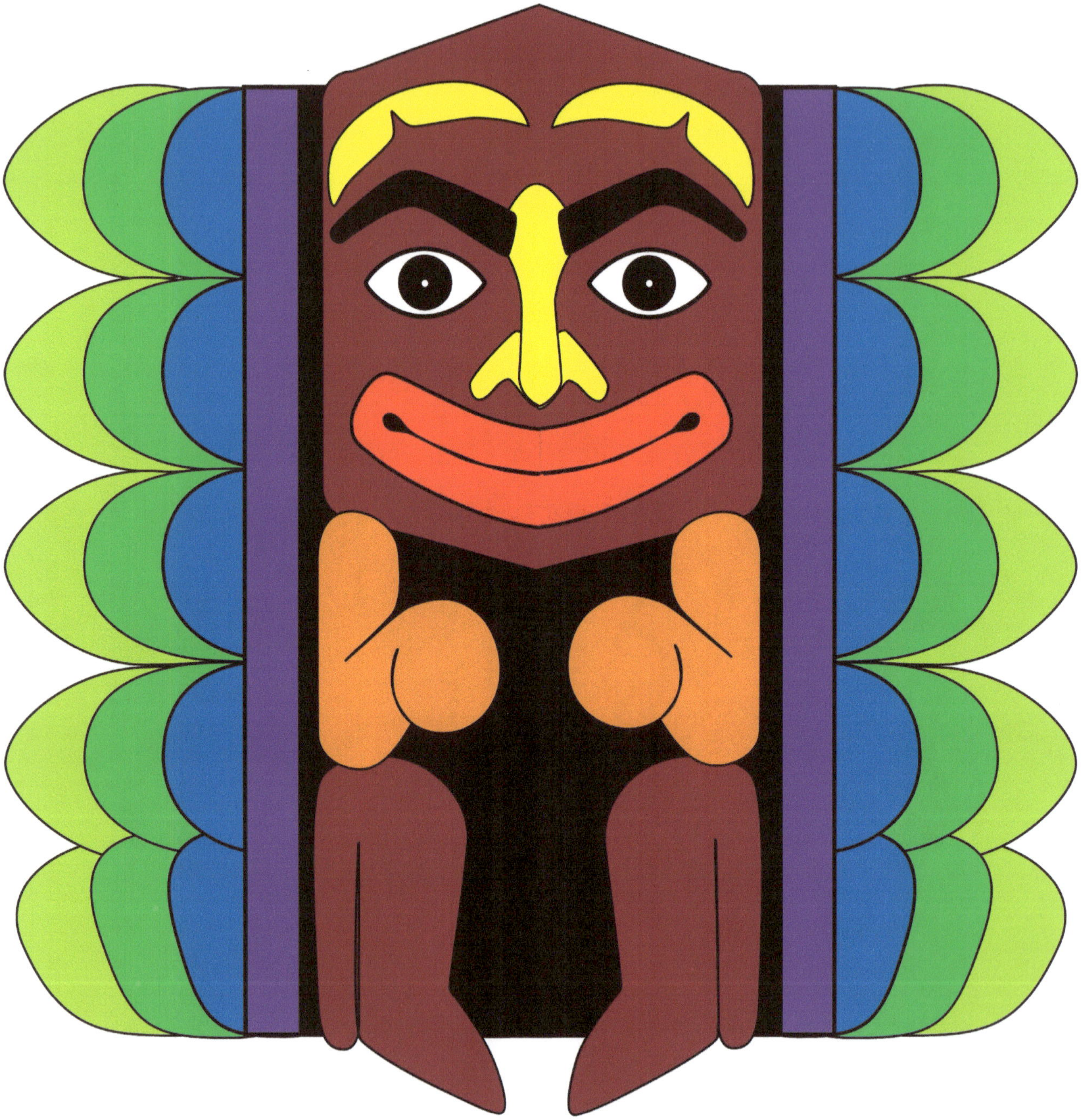

Dance Frontlet, carved and painted on wood
representing a bear. Tlingit Tribe, Northwest Coast, late 19th Century.

American Indian Art

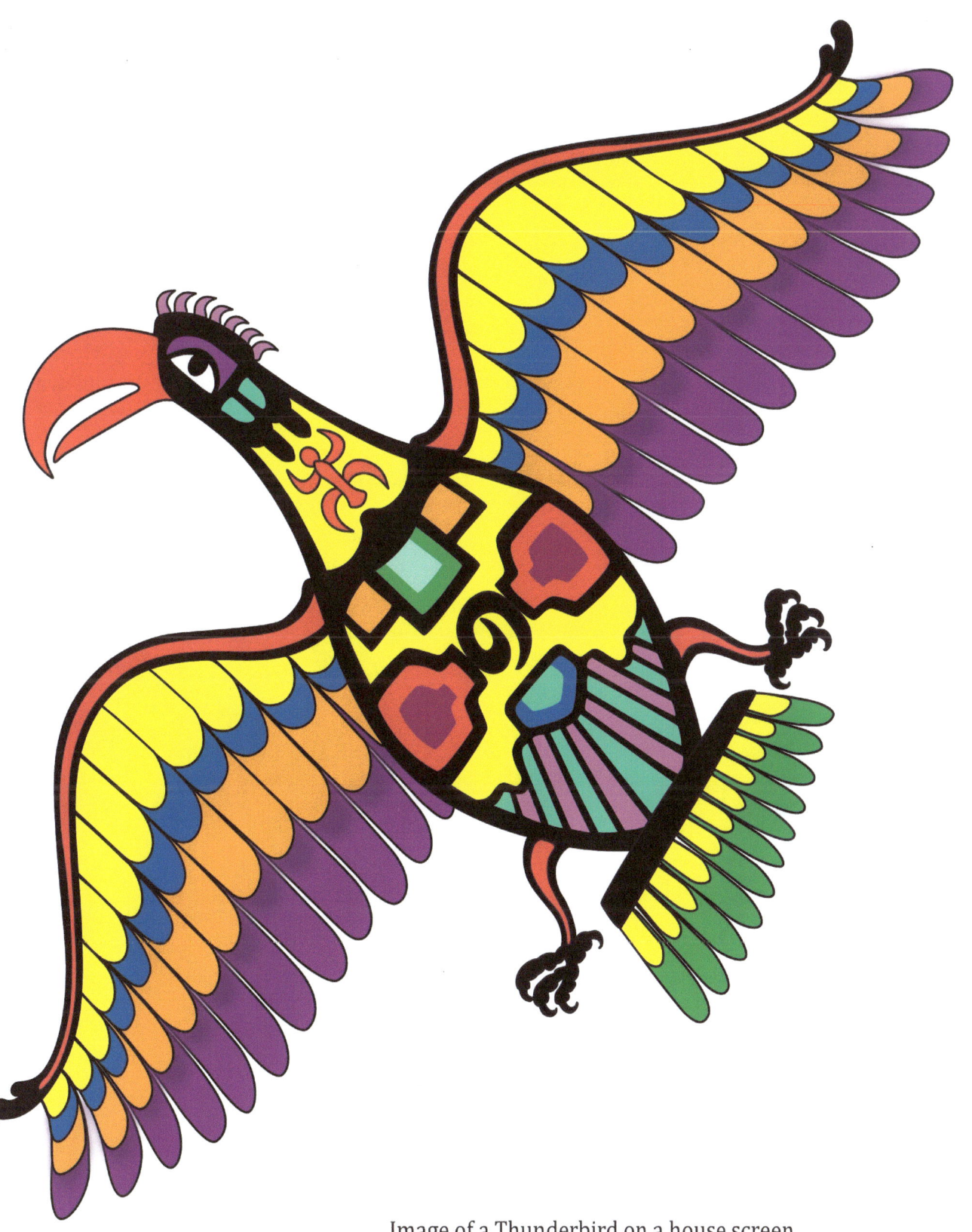

Image of a Thunderbird on a house screen,
displayed at potlatches and other significant occasions.
Western Canada, 1850 C.E.

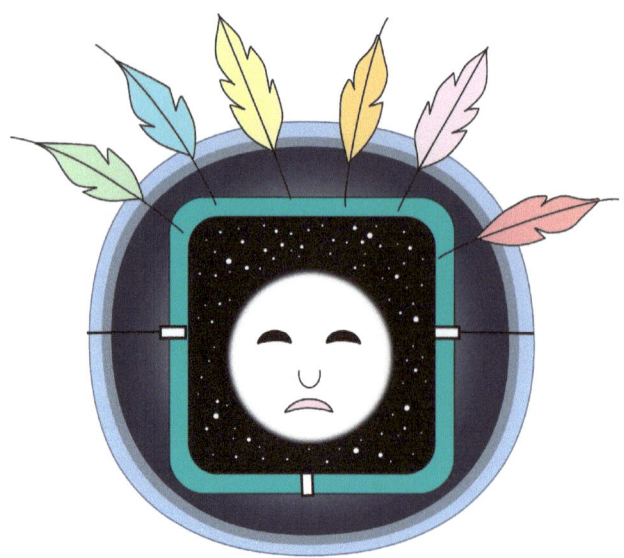

Inuit Cosmology: Face represents the important spirit of the moon. Surrounding hoops are different layers of the Universe, and feathers represent the stars in the Heaven.

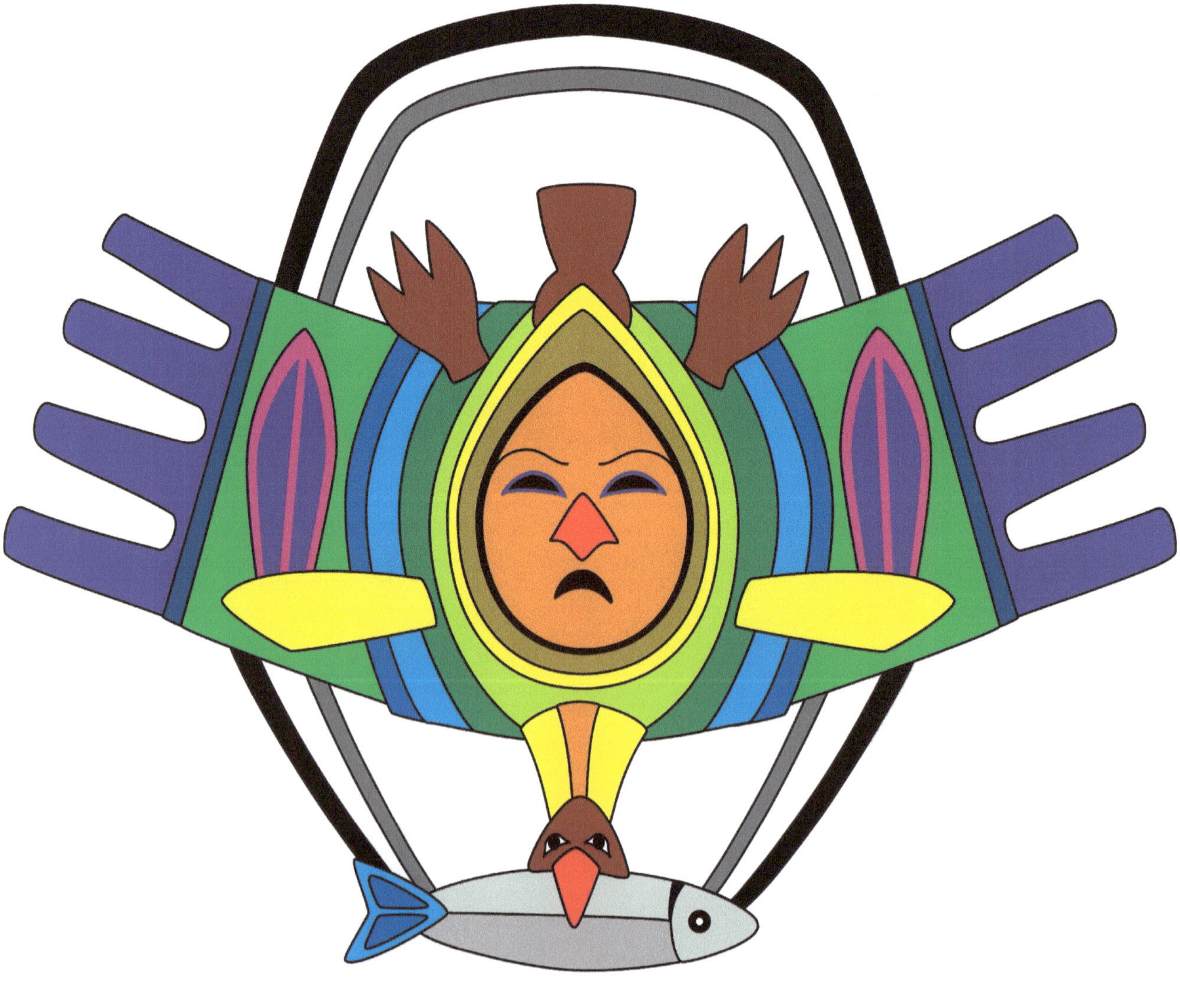

Eskimos in Goodnews Bay and in Hooper Bay (Alaska) wore this mask. It represents a falcon holding a fish.

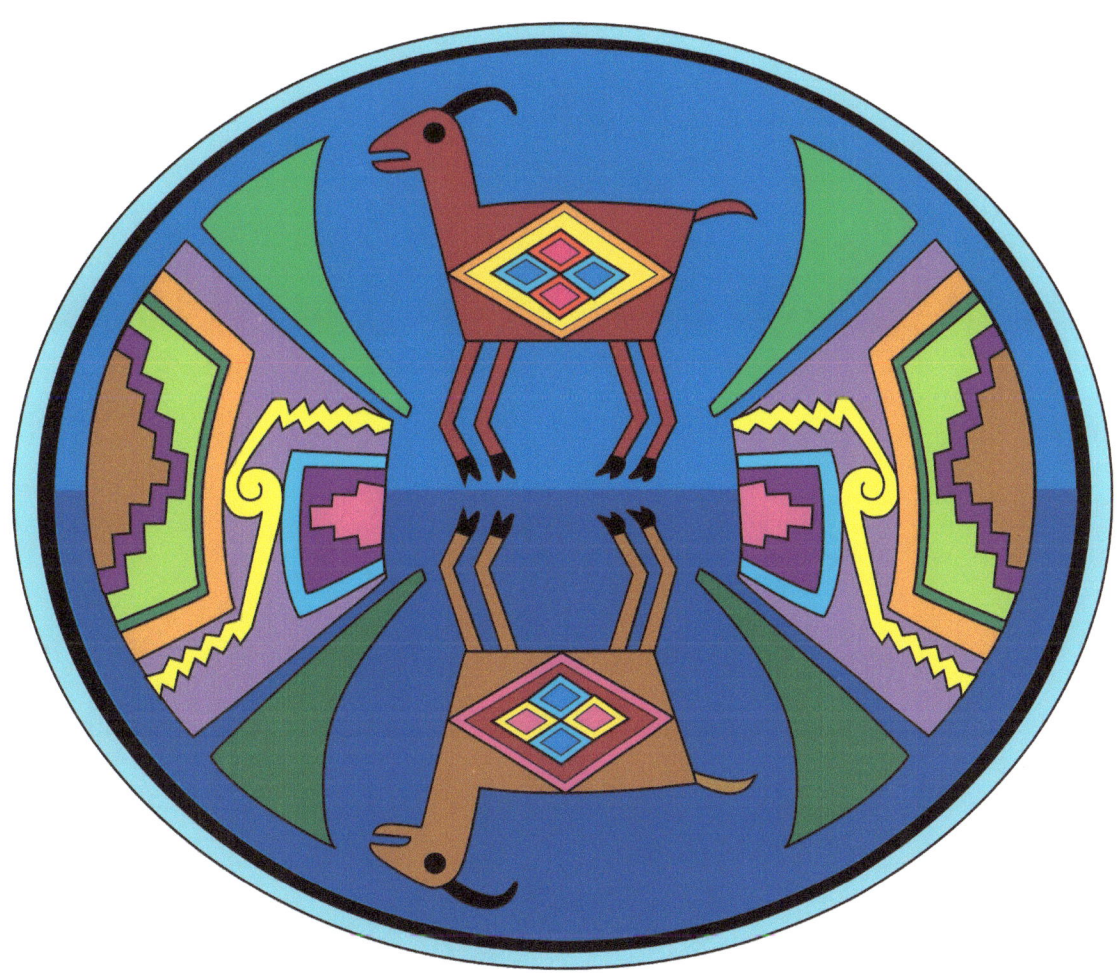

Highly stylized drawing of Mountain Goat and other elements on a bowl
by Mimbres potter. New Mexico, USA. Southwestern pottery paintings existed even before 1200 B.C.E.

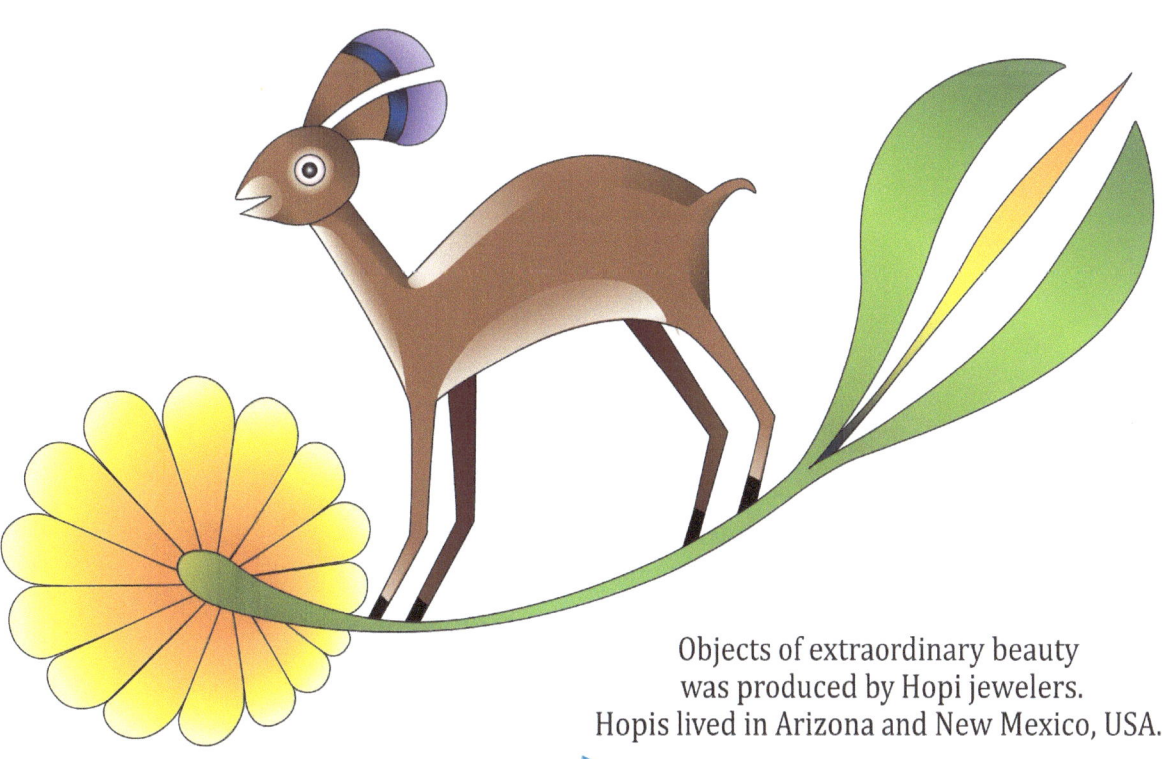

Objects of extraordinary beauty
was produced by Hopi jewelers.
Hopis lived in Arizona and New Mexico, USA.

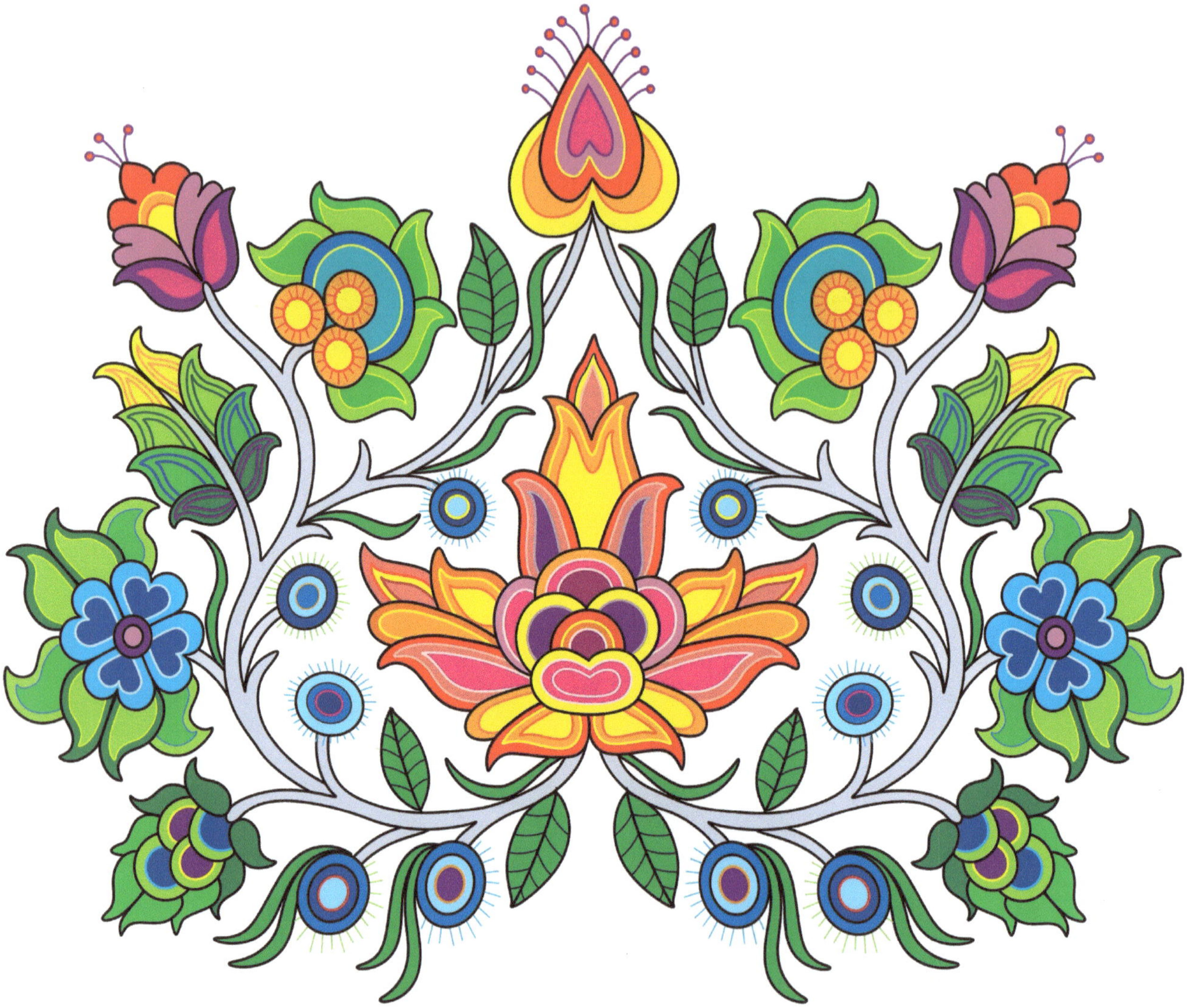

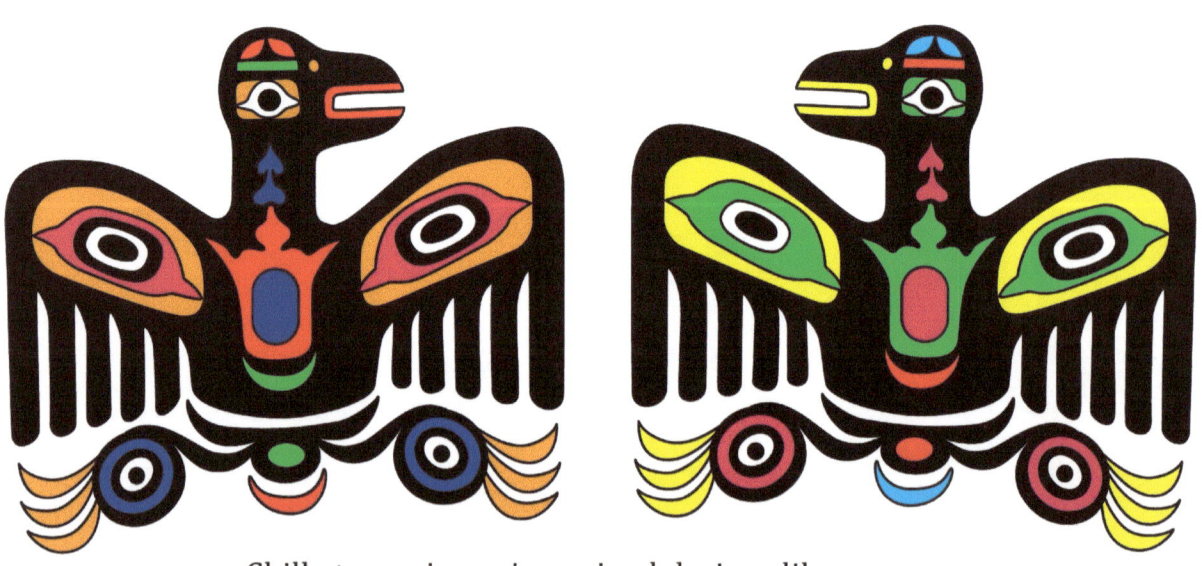

Floral designs on men's leggings. Floral motifs replaced
earlier geometric and spirit designs in Woodlands art during 19th Century C.E.

Chilkat weaving using animal designs like raven.

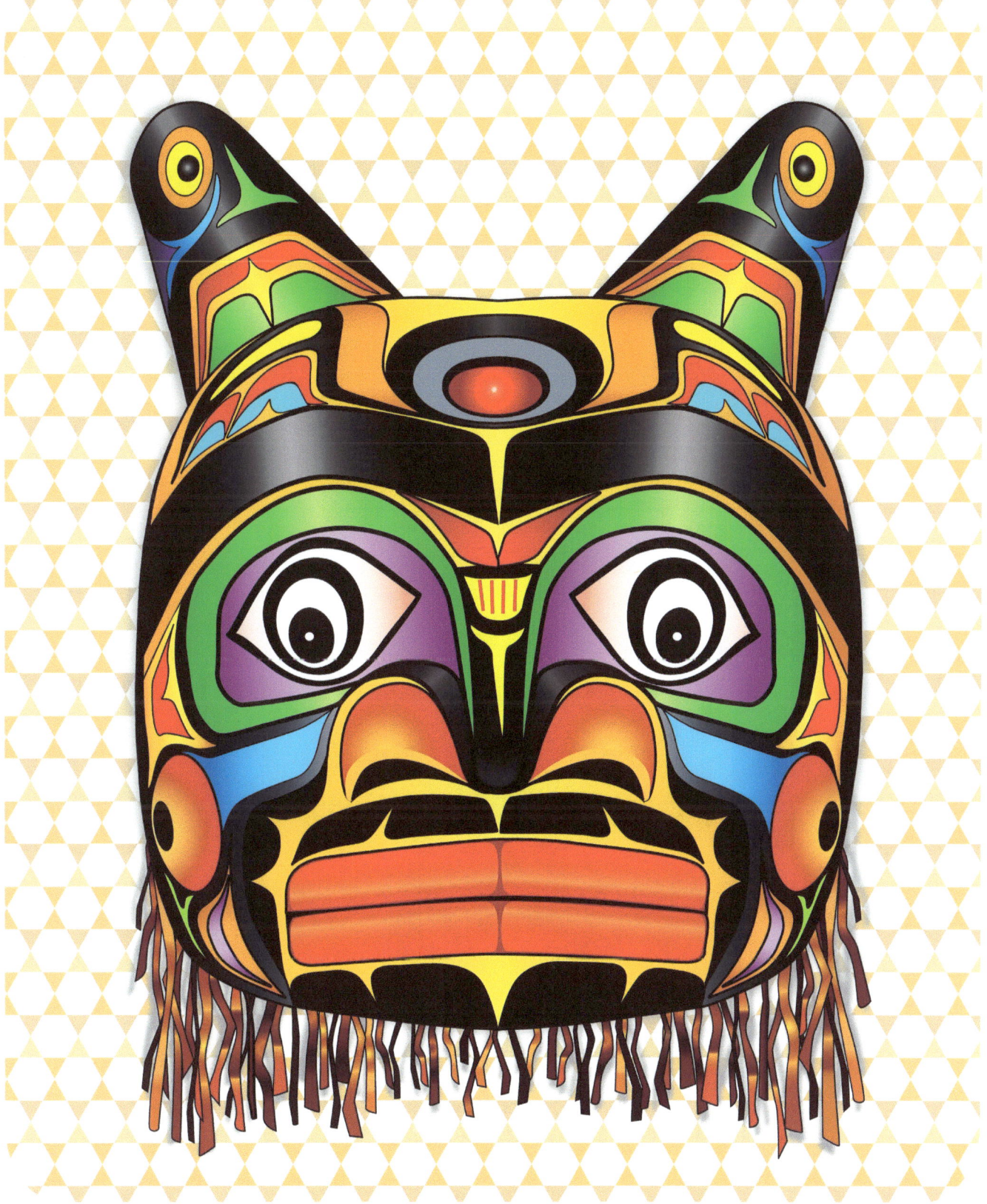

Sea Monster Mask

The mask represents a specific sea monster who came out of the sea
to build a house, assisted by a Thunderbird. Western Canada.

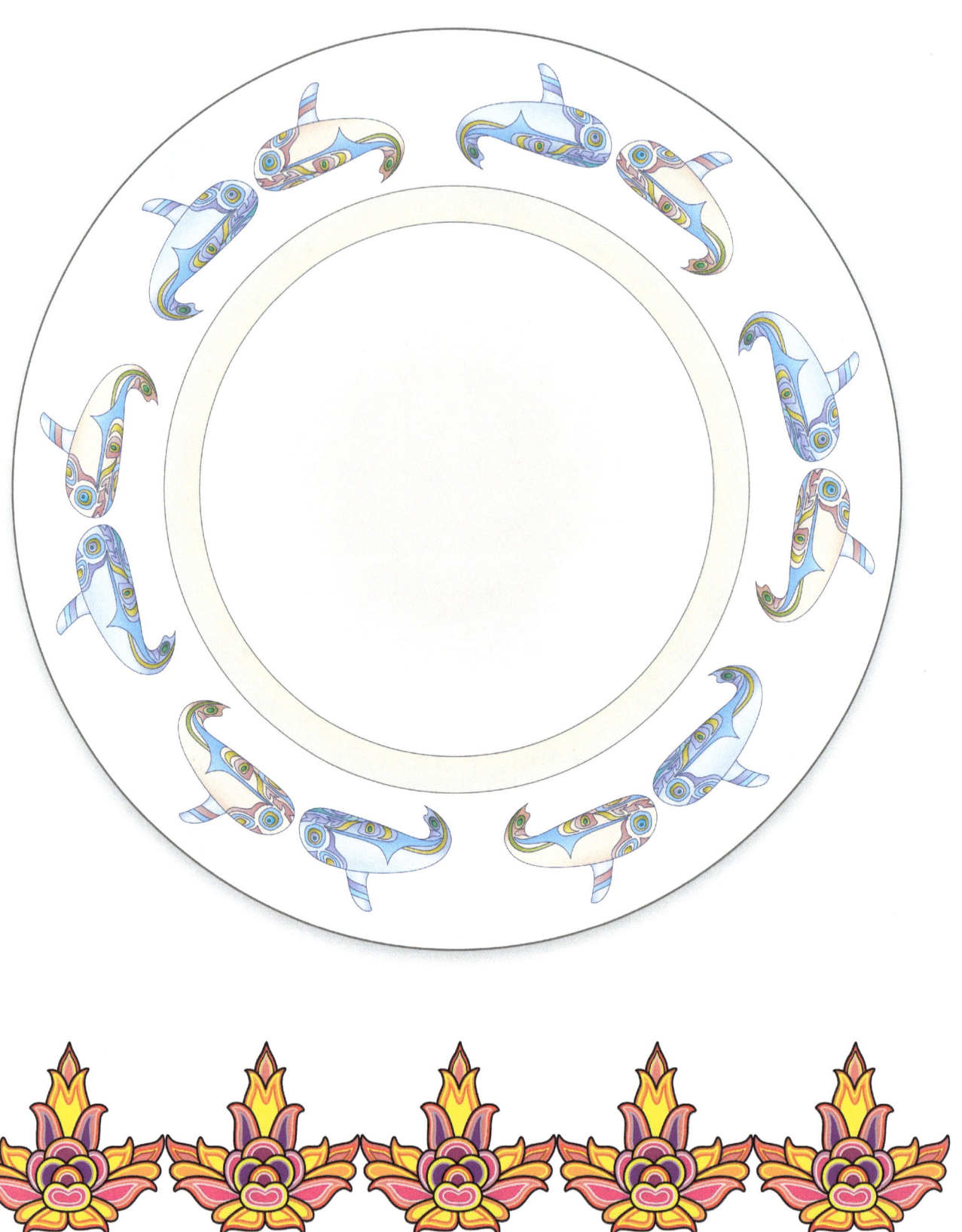

Examples of images created using the elements found in American Indian Art.

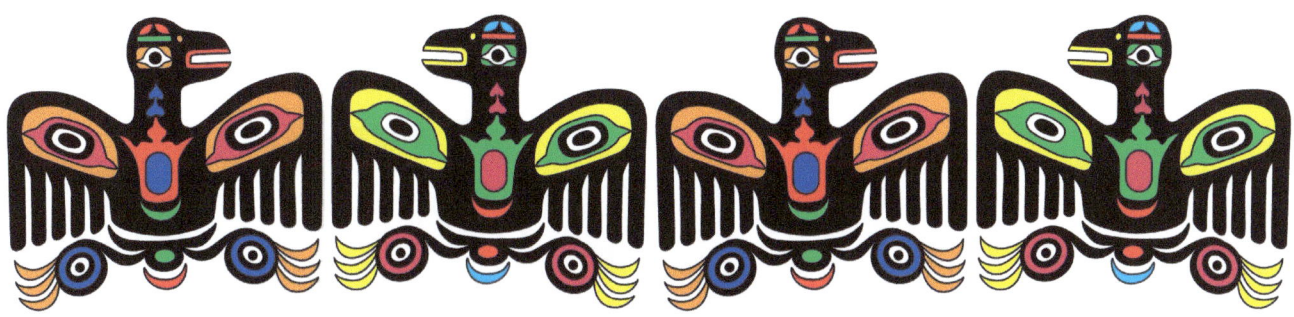

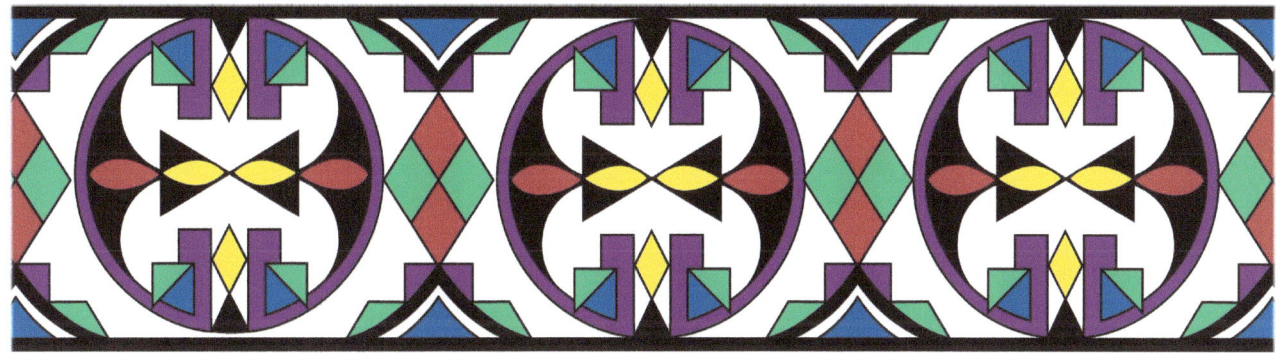

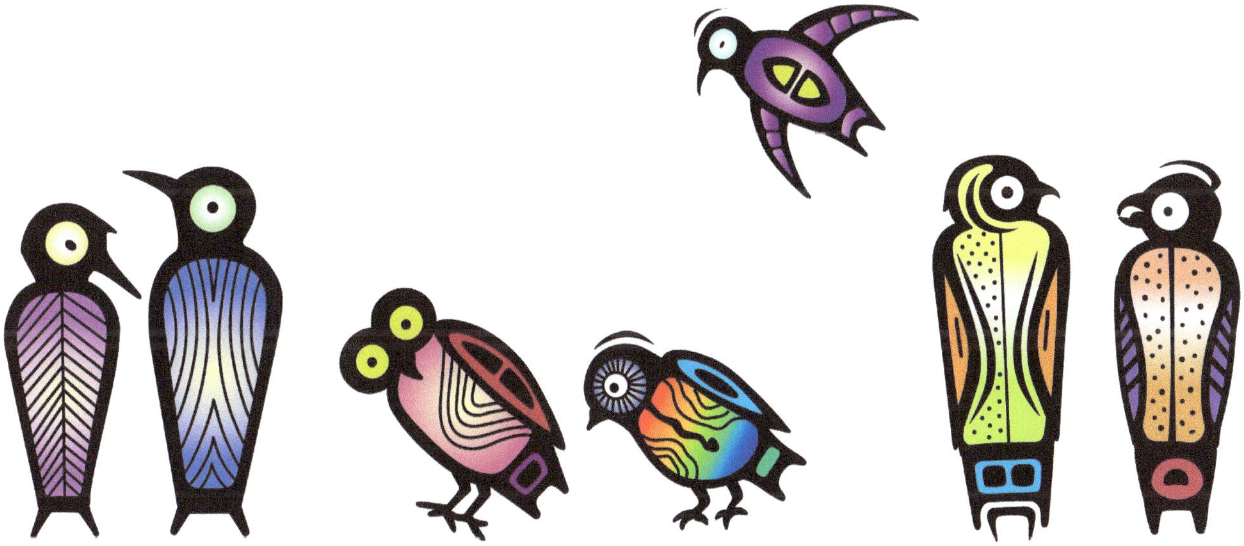

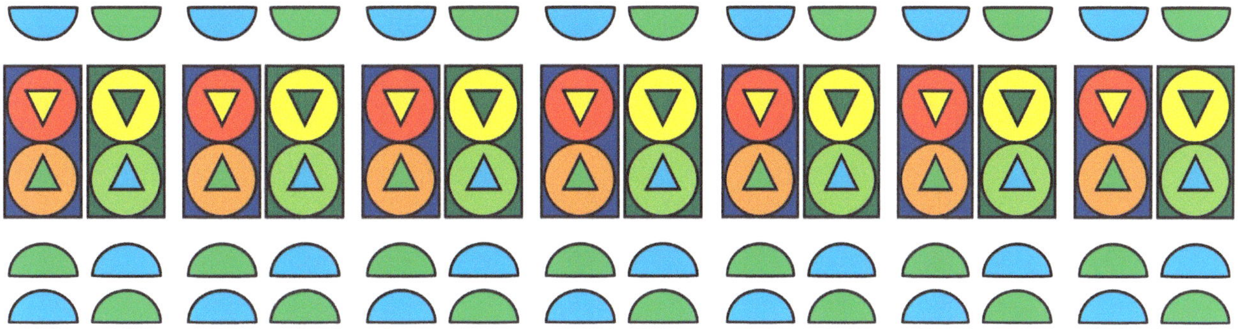

Examples of images created using the elements found in American Indian Art.

A LOOK INTO
Pre-Columbian Art

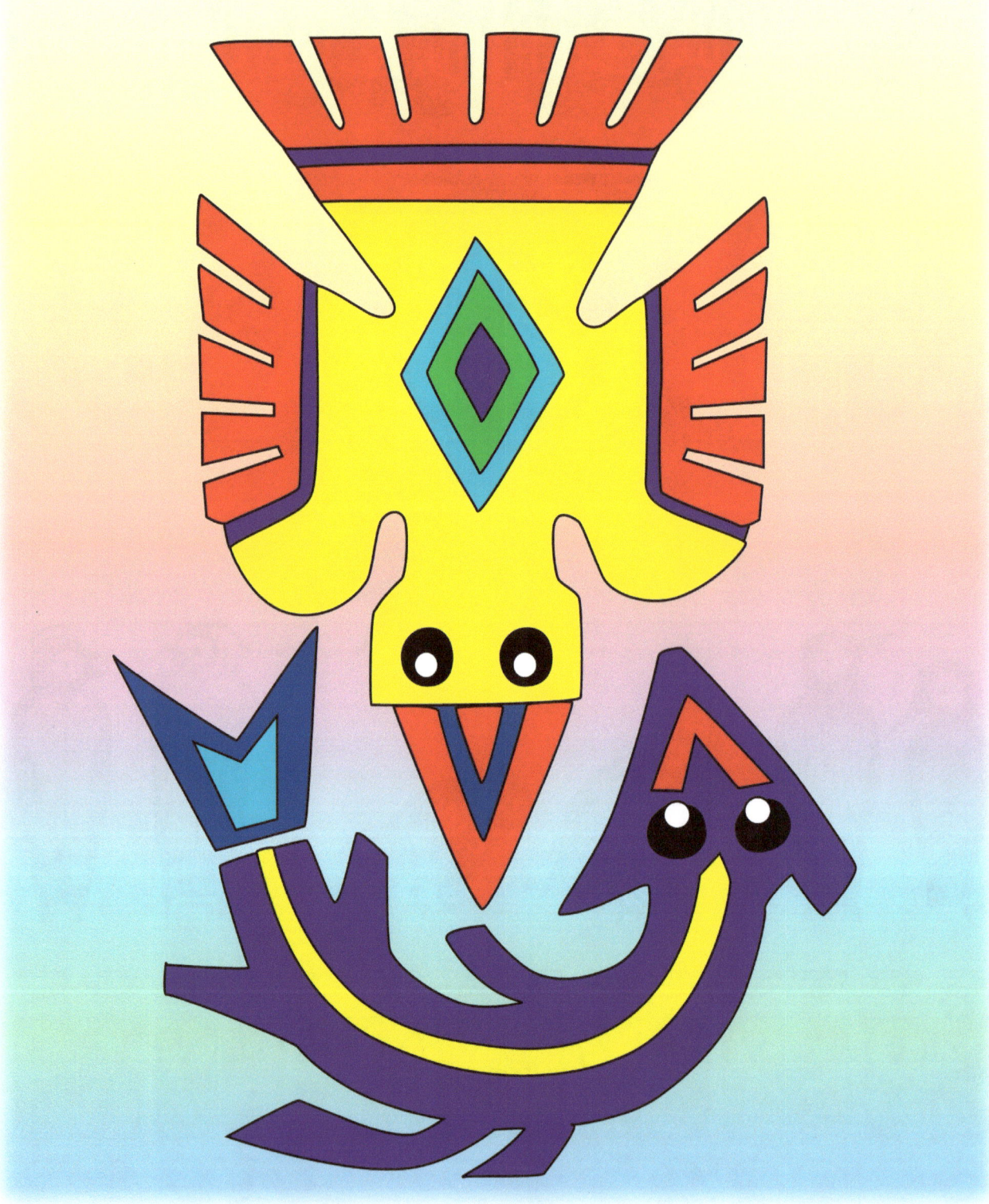

Shrouds found in Paracas, South America, are over 2000 years old and are still vivid in colors. Human figures, deities, mythological animals such as Jaguar, Surpent Dragon, and others are depicted on plain or checkered background.

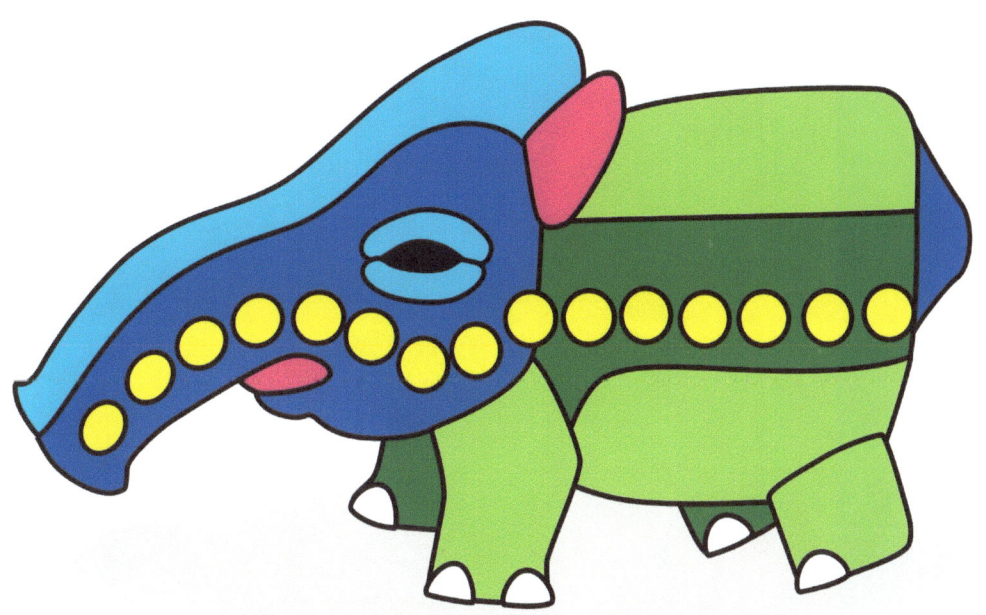

Ocarina in the form of a tapir. Northern Guatemala highlands.

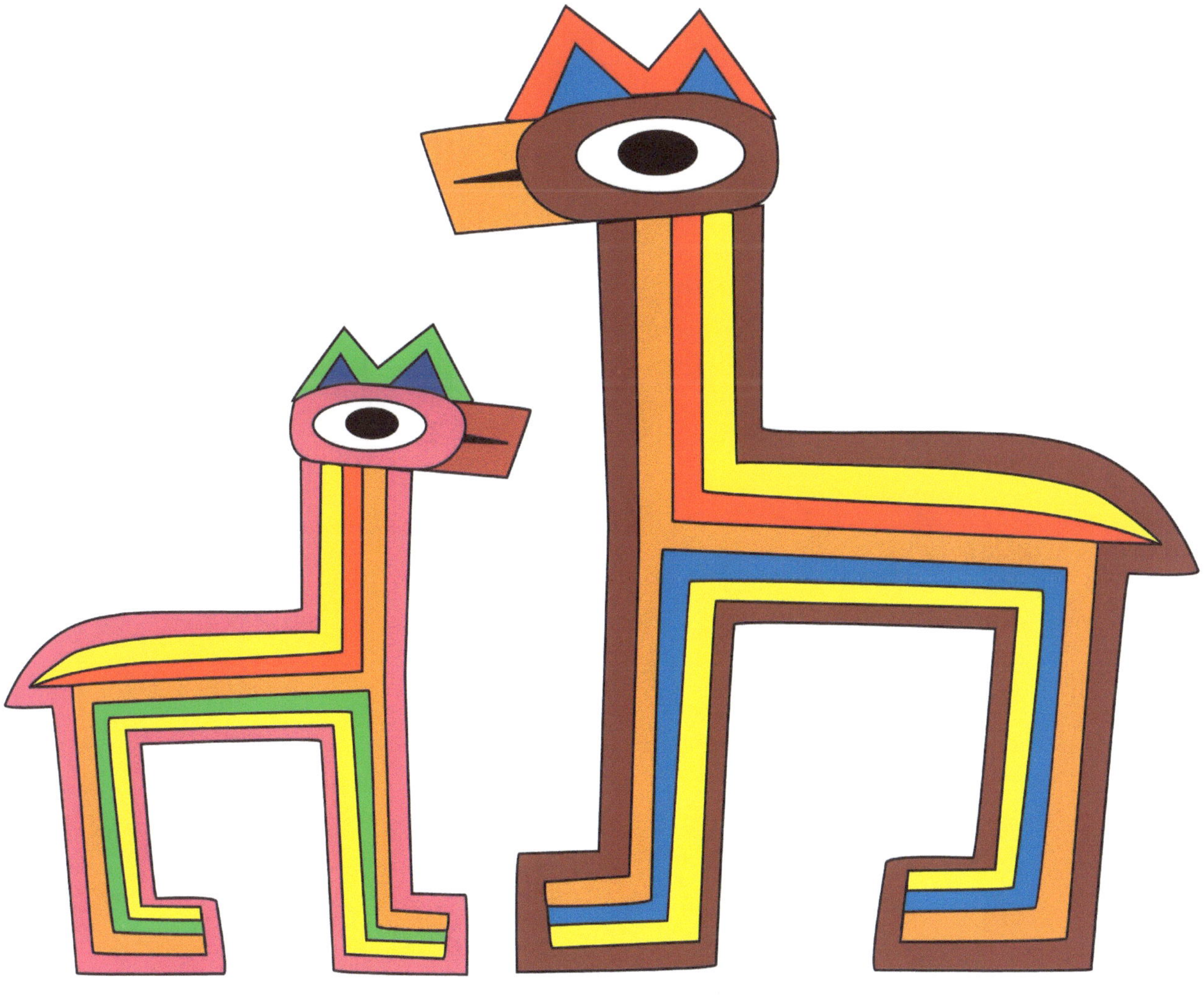

Incas created superb patterns, such as this highly abstract shape of a llama. Saksaywaman, Peru.

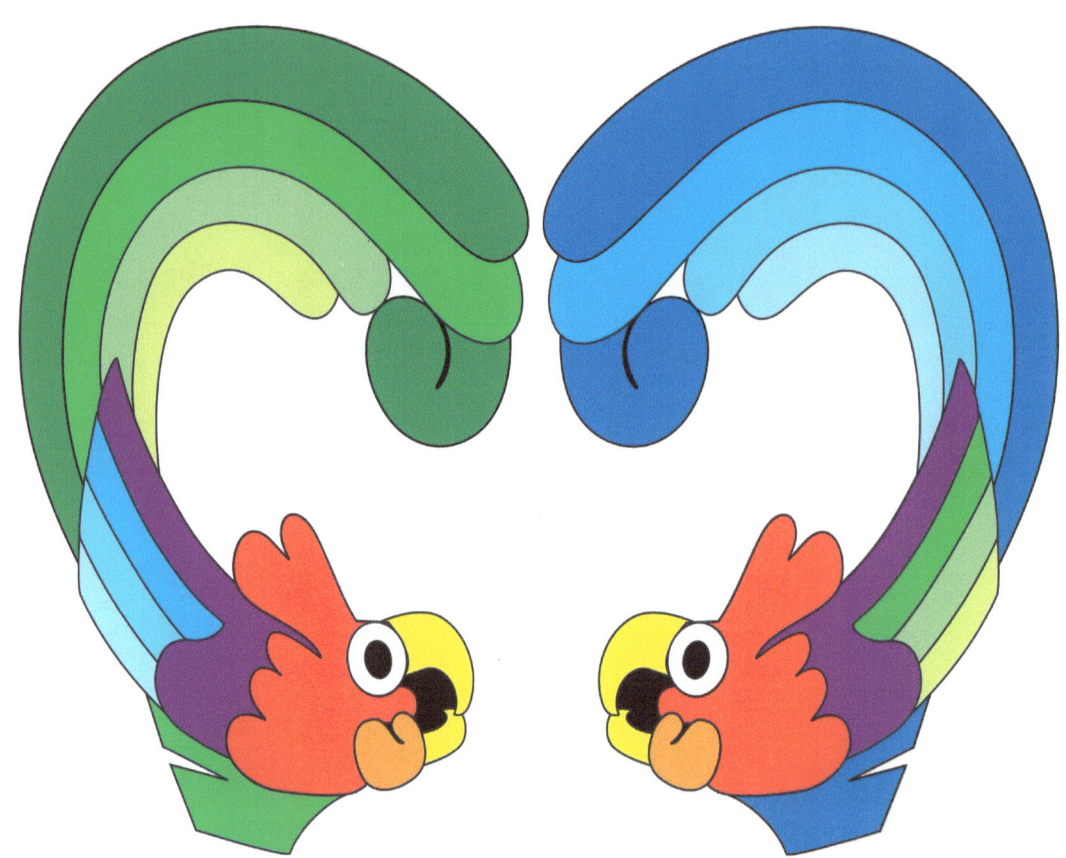

'Great Sun' or Quetzal Macaw, Mayan Civilization.

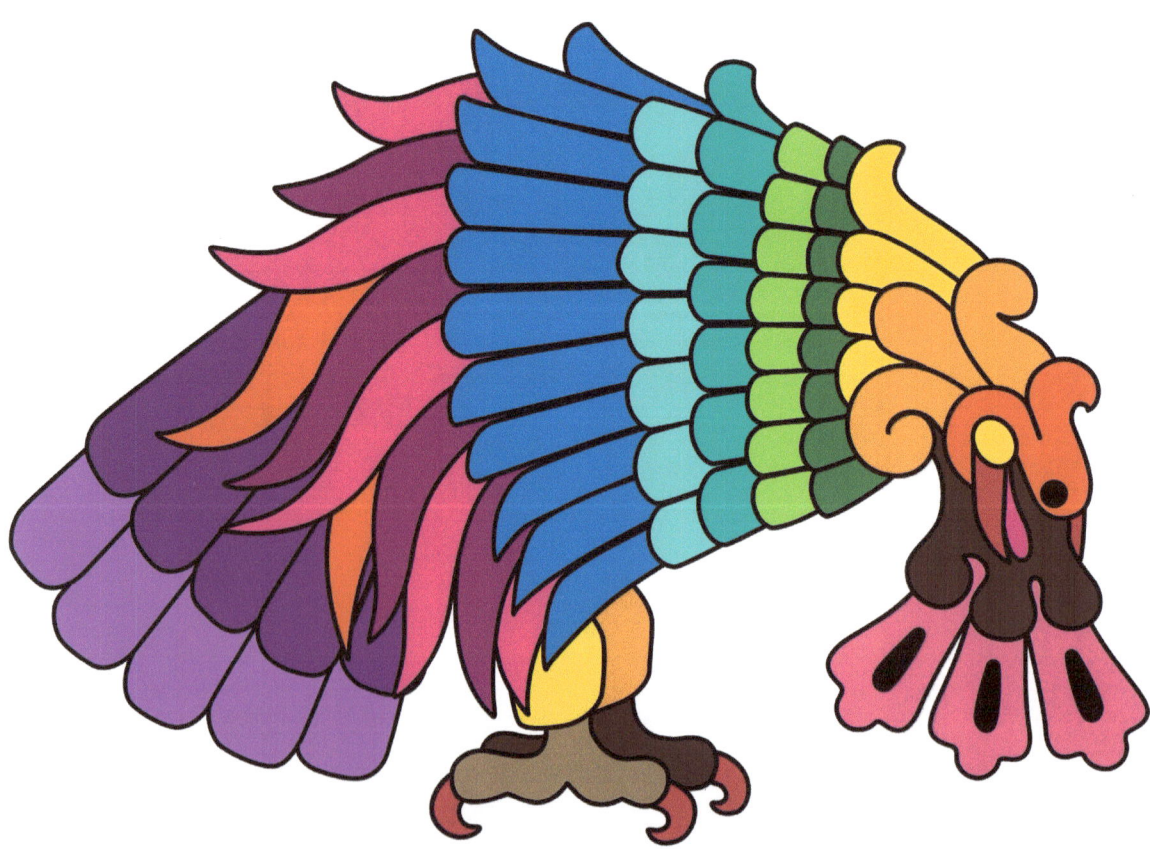

Eagle on a frieze in the temple of Quetzalcoatl, Tula.

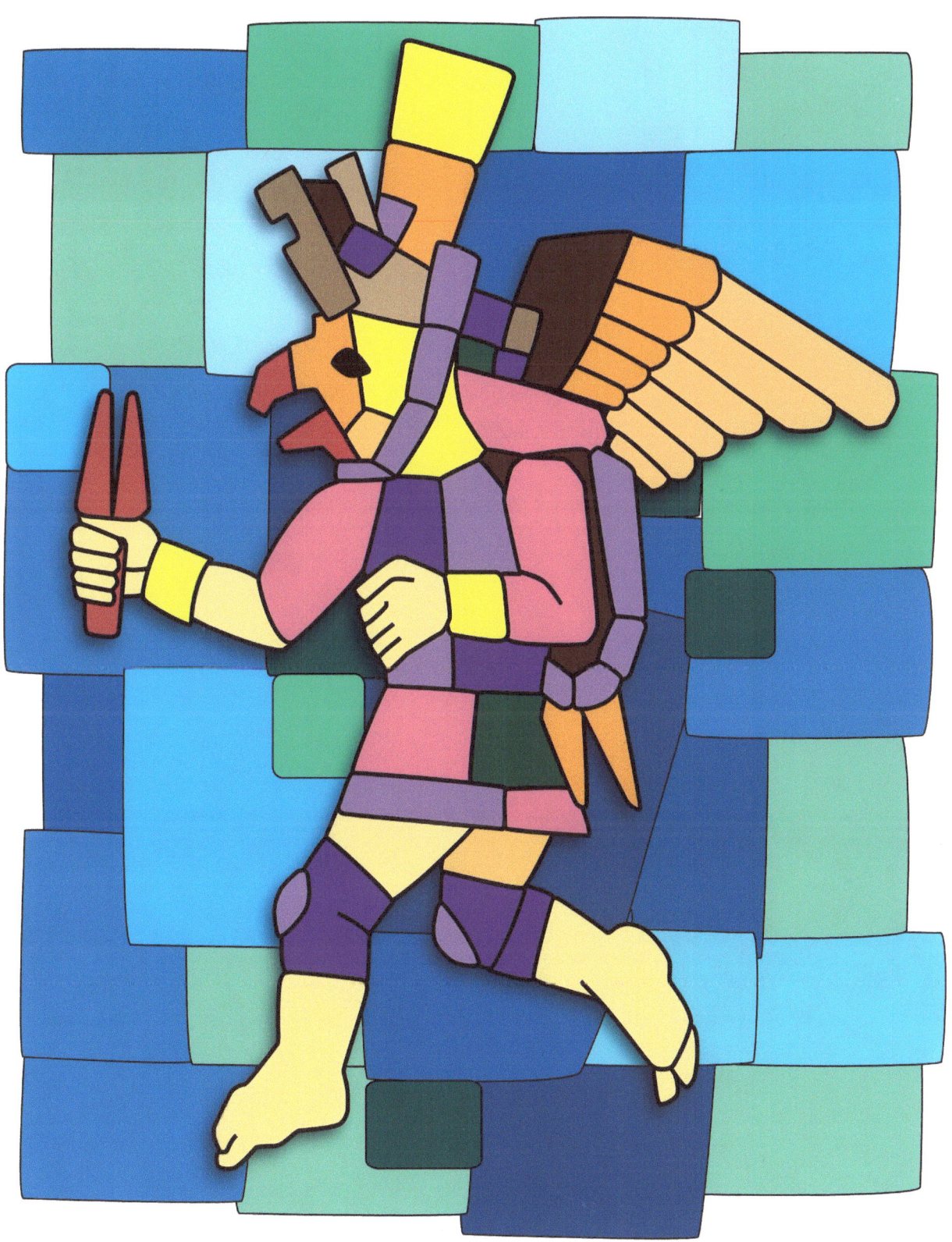

Found on a pair of Moche earplugs with bean runners.
Peru, 300 - 600 C.E. Gold with turquoise and shell inlay.

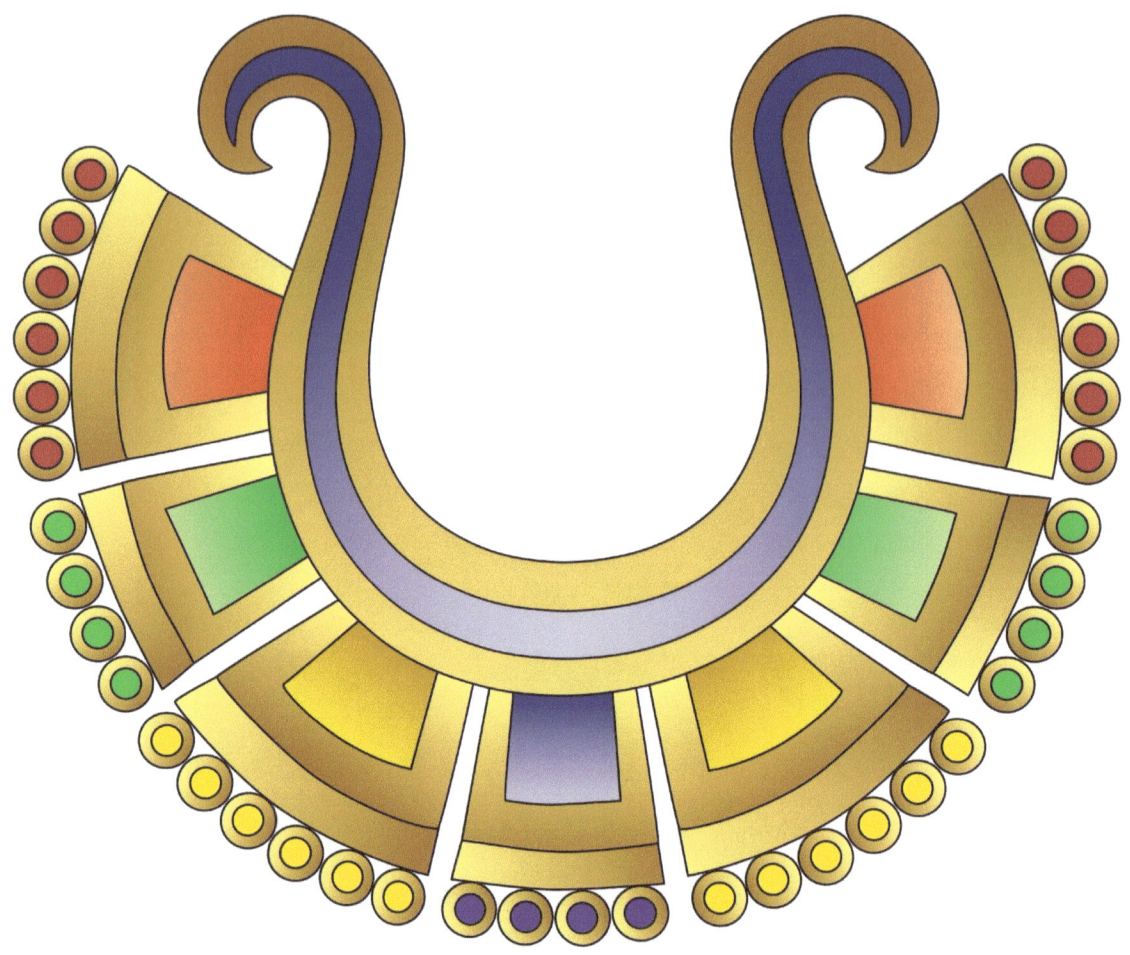

In the moneyless society of the Aztecs, gold and silver symbolized wealth. This is an Aztec necklace.

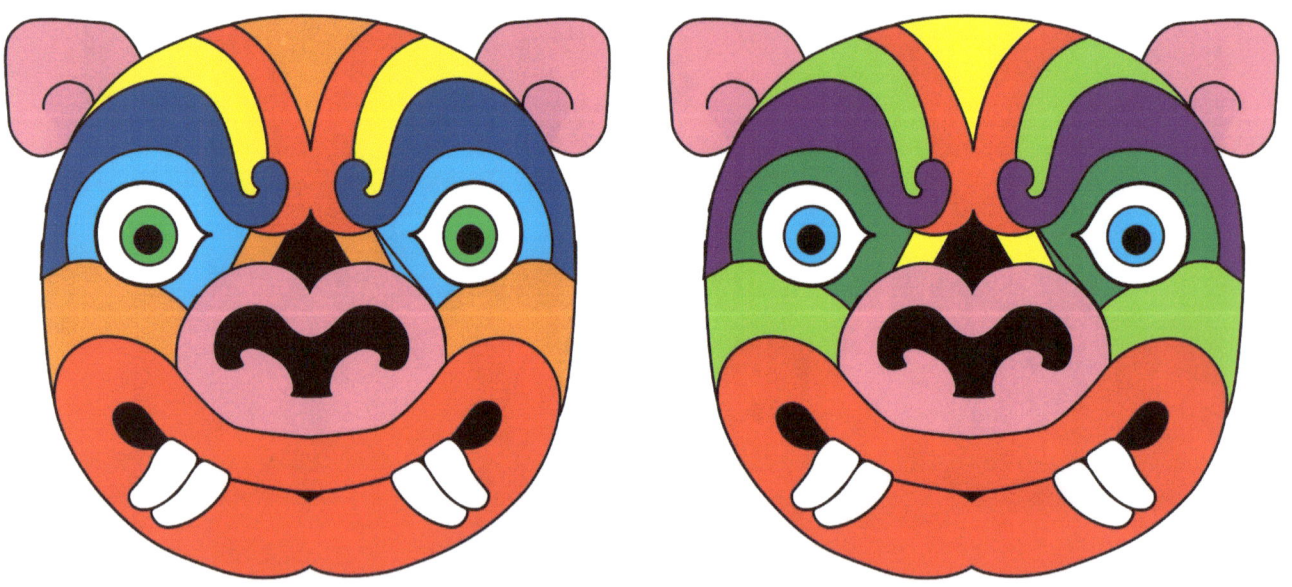

Were-Jaguar tenoned into the wall of the pyramid of Chavin.
It is the earliest stone temple found in Peru (Olmec mythology).

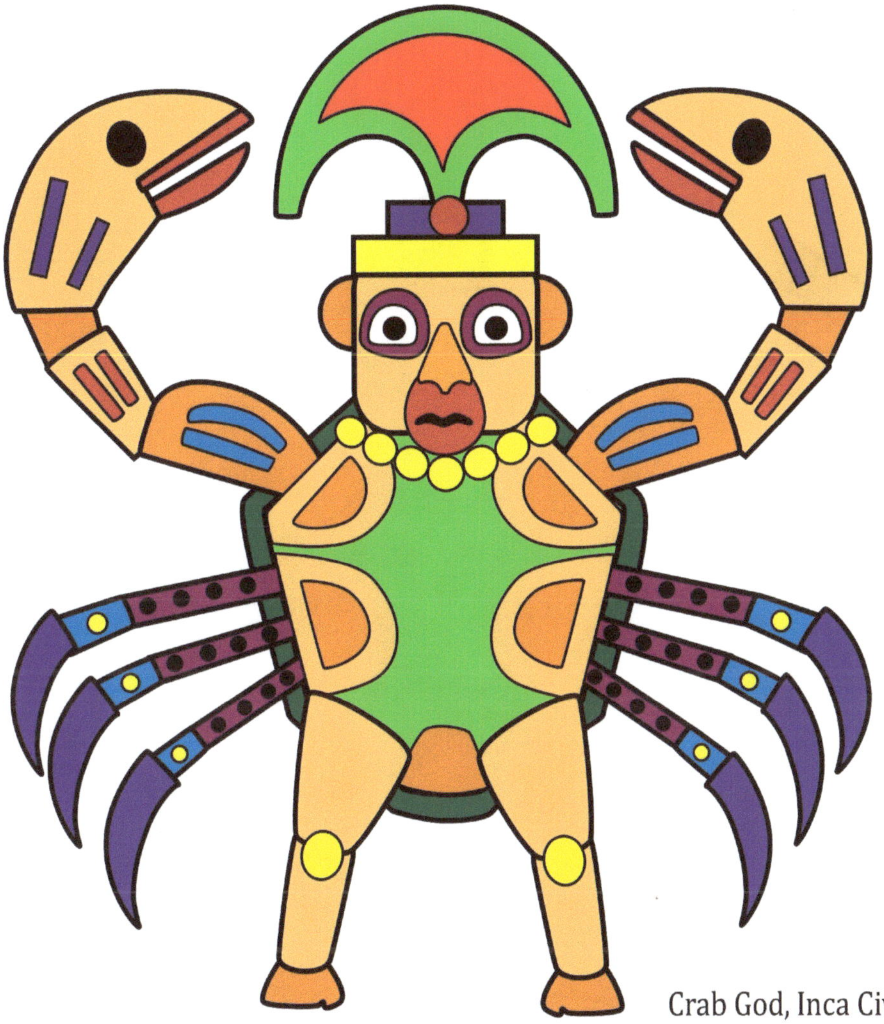

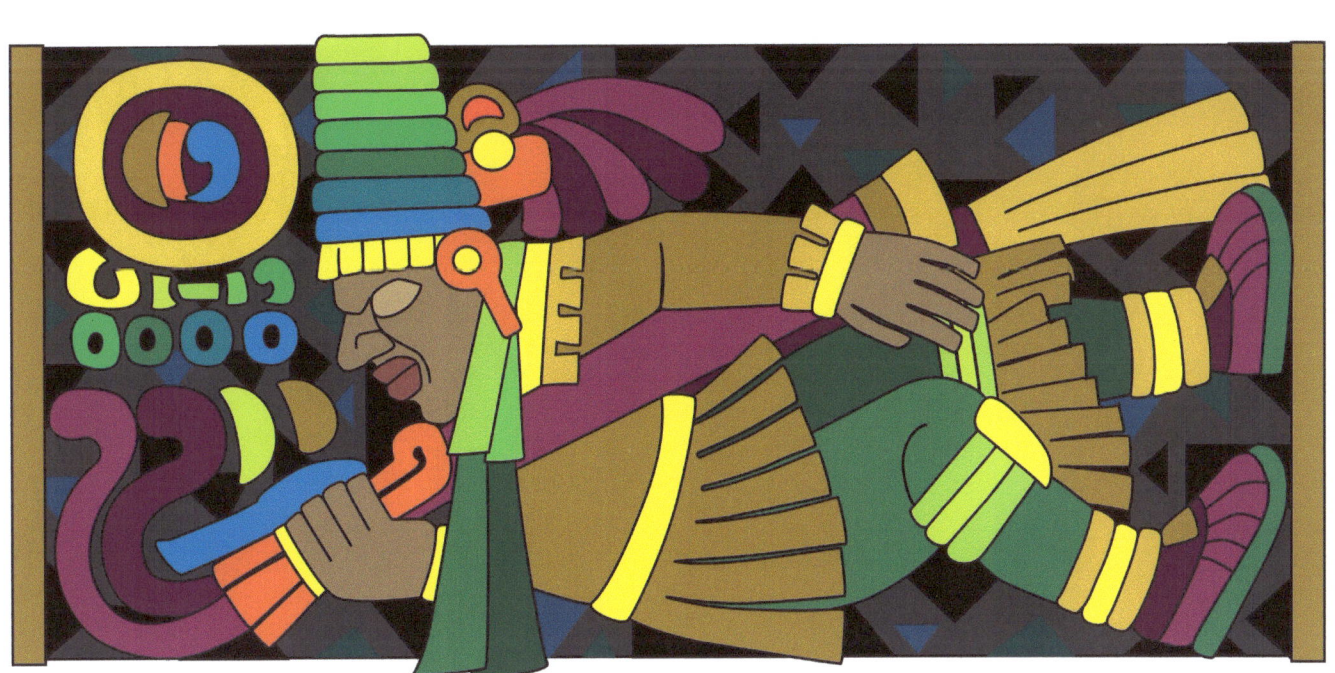

Crab God, Inca Civilization, Peru.

Toltec warrior, Tula, Mexico.

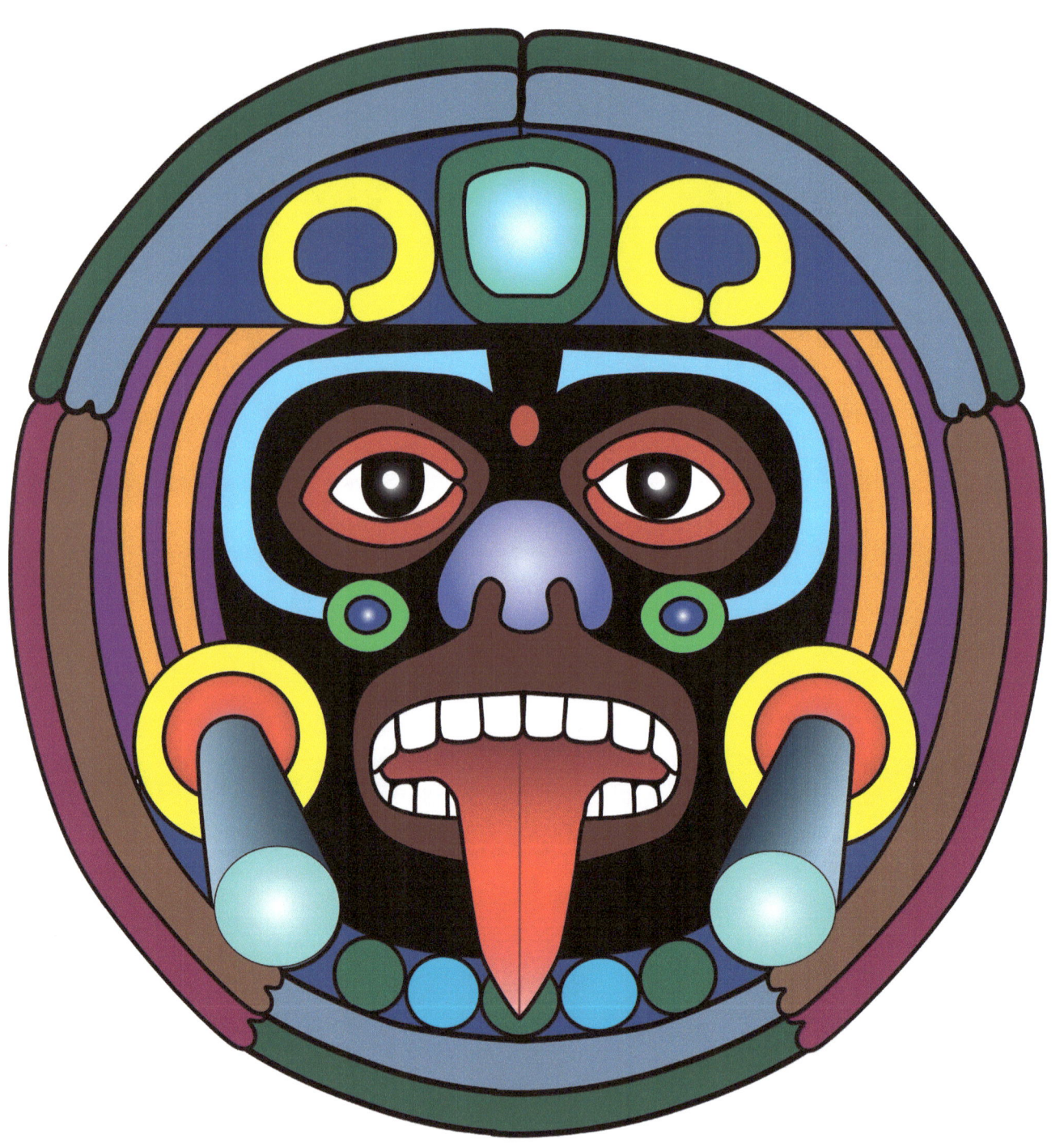

Part of an Aztec Relic. Intricately carved circular stone. The Relic is 4 feet in diameter and weighs 24 tons. Face of the Sun God. Carved in 986 C.E.

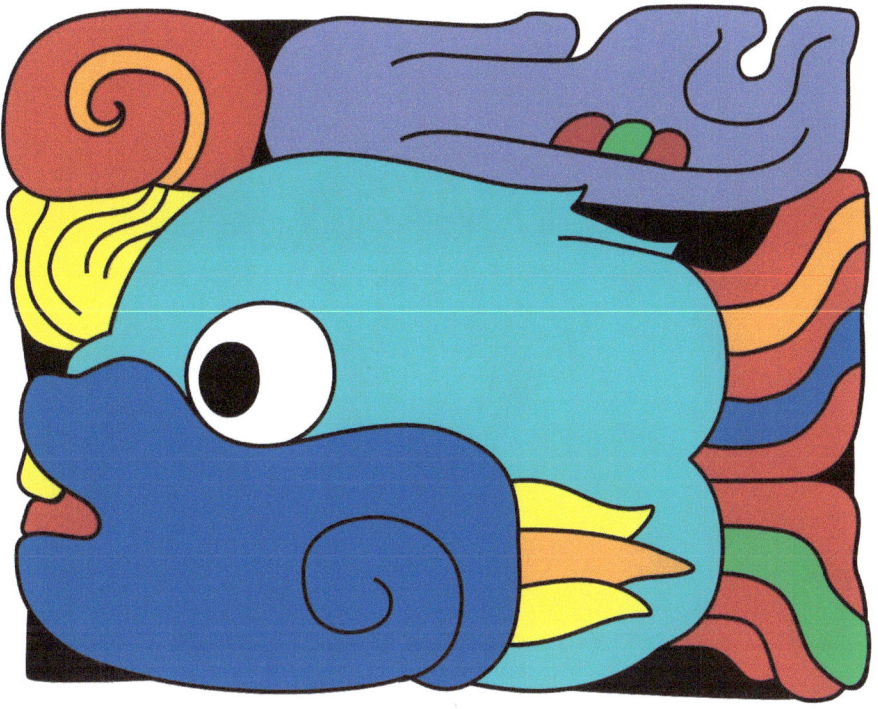

A large hieroglyph representing place and name,
from Structure 10L - 22A (The Mat House). Copan Civilization.

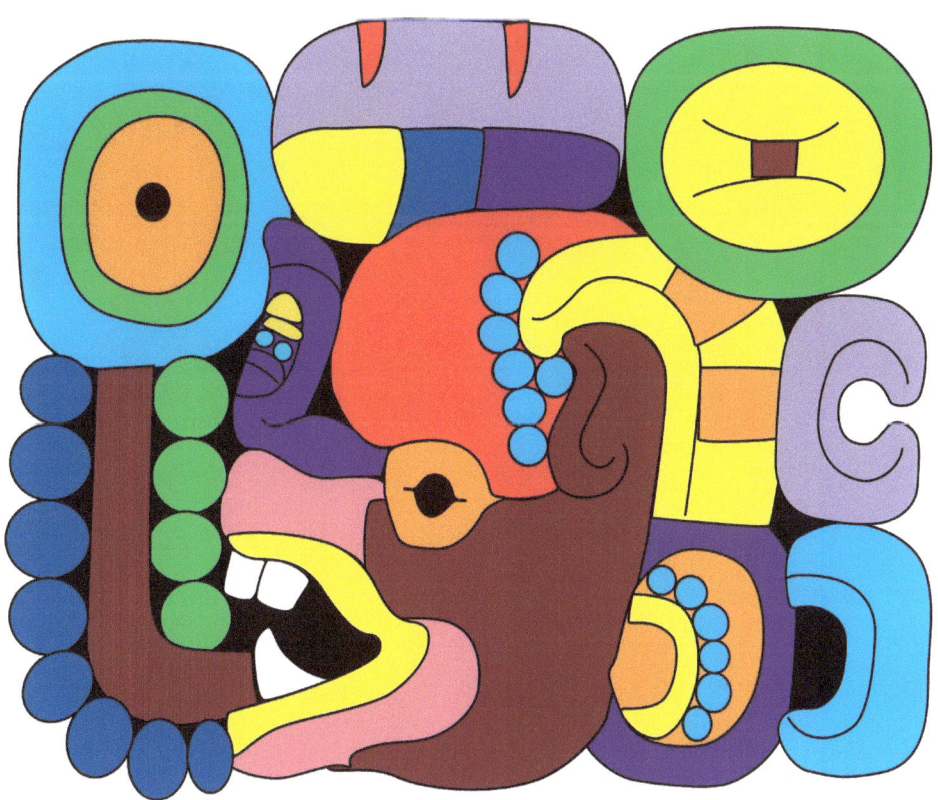

The Copan emblem-glyph. The beads on the left represent sacred drops. Two signs on the top signify the person as the Holy Lord of the kingdom. The kingdom is named by the sign of a leaf-nosed bat as shown.

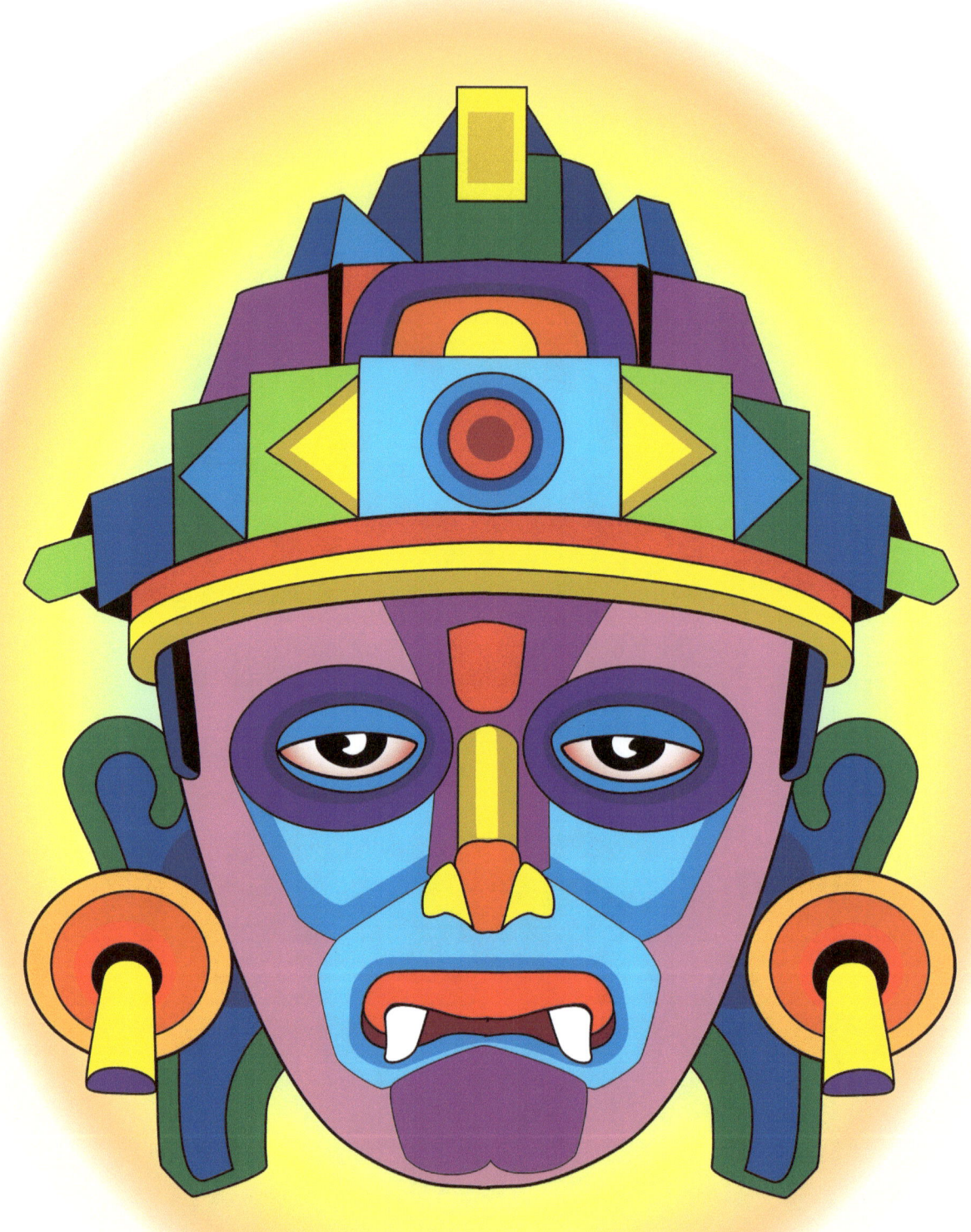

Tlaloc, the Rain God. Artists have given him a gentle spring shower
as well as devastating storm. Found at Mayapan.

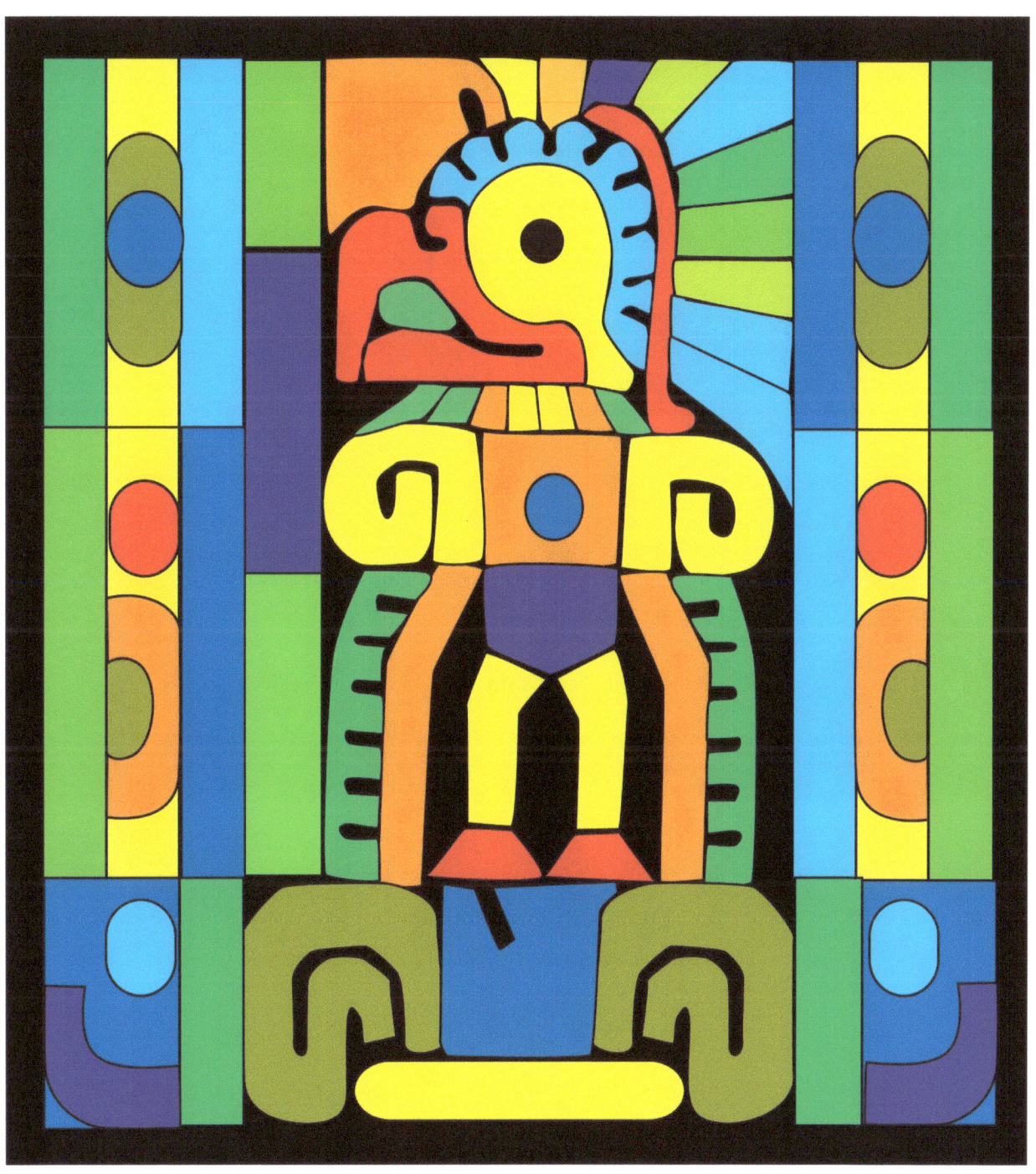

Low relief decorating the Quetzalpapalotl Palace. Side view of a Quetzal bird.

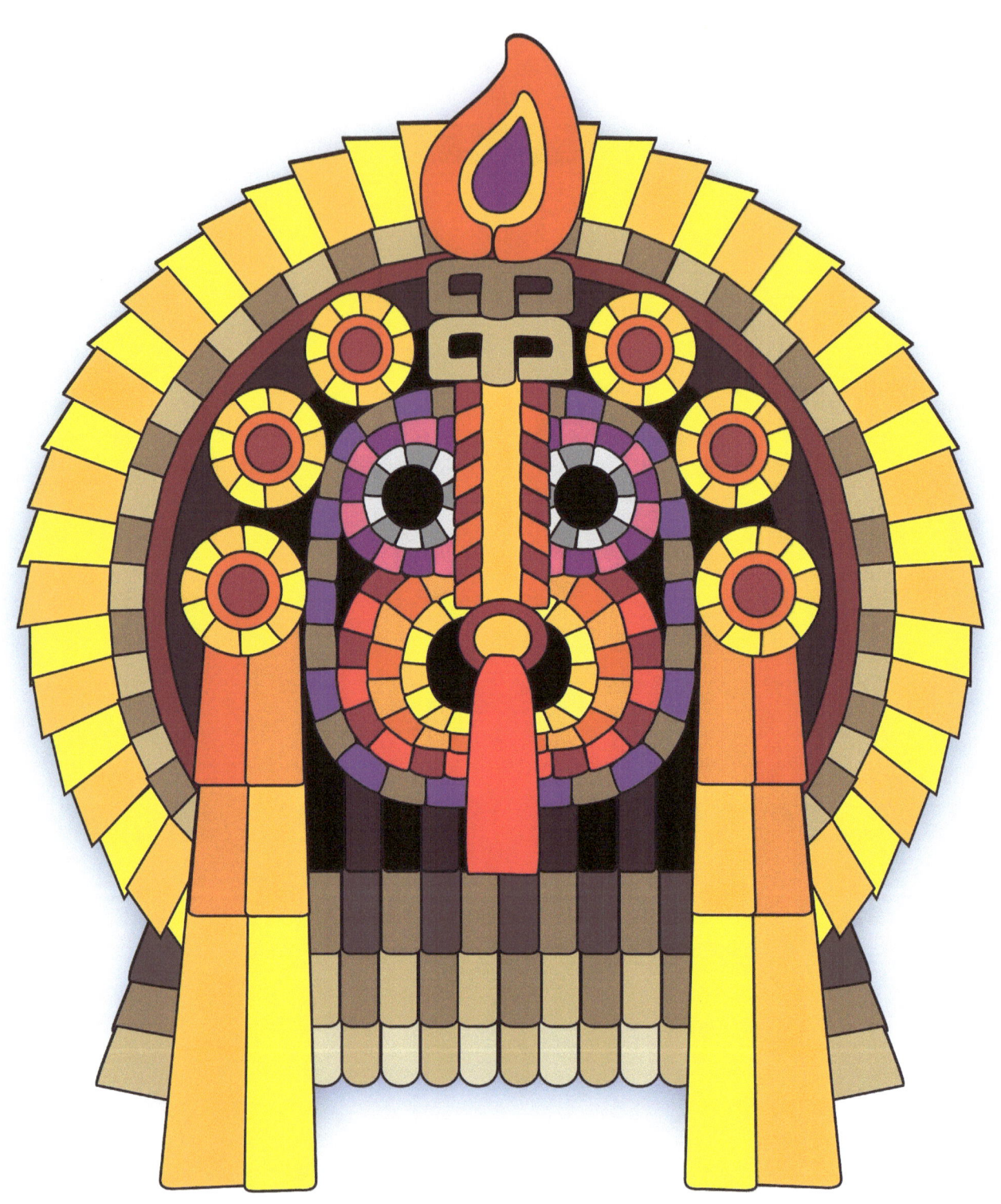

Uxmal, Mexico. Between 800 - 900 C.E.
A stylized head of a ruler as indicated by the elaborated ornaments.

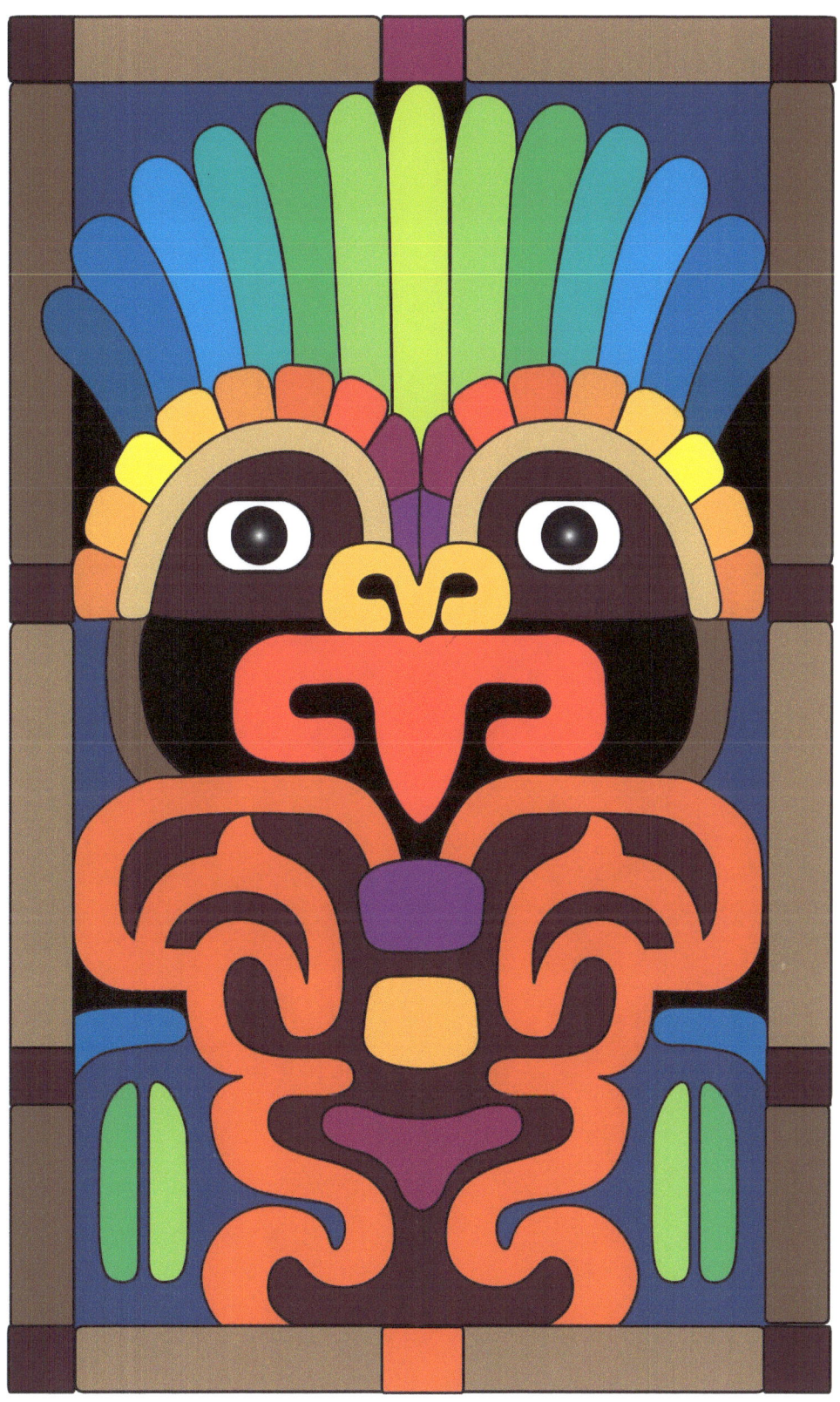

Bizarre imagery of the hybrid god, both bird and butterfly.
Uxmal, Mexico. 800 - 900 C.E.

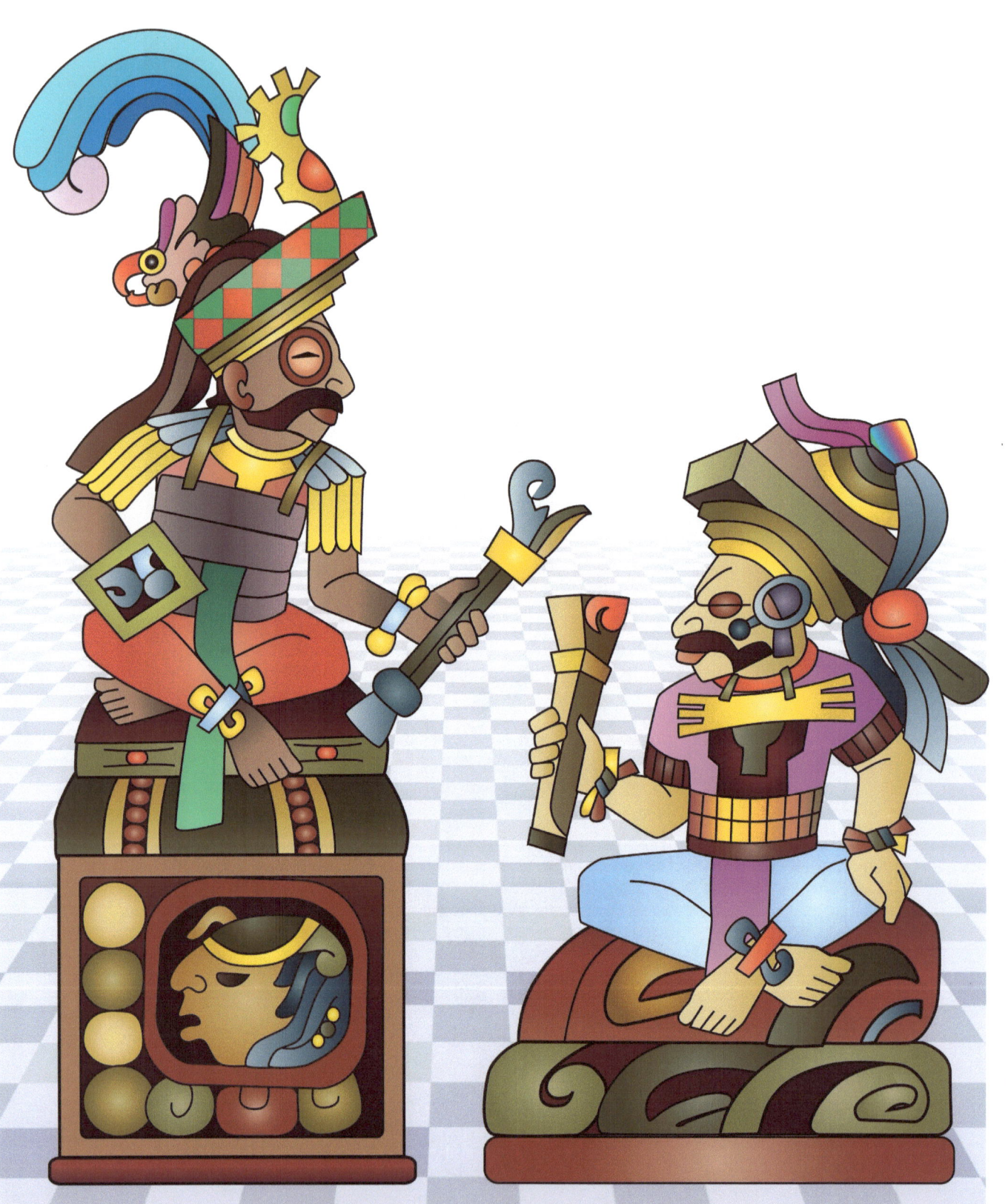

Relief on stone representing Copan Dynasty rulers. Middle of 7th Century C.E. Dates and names of the rulers have been identified deciphering the hieroglyphics.

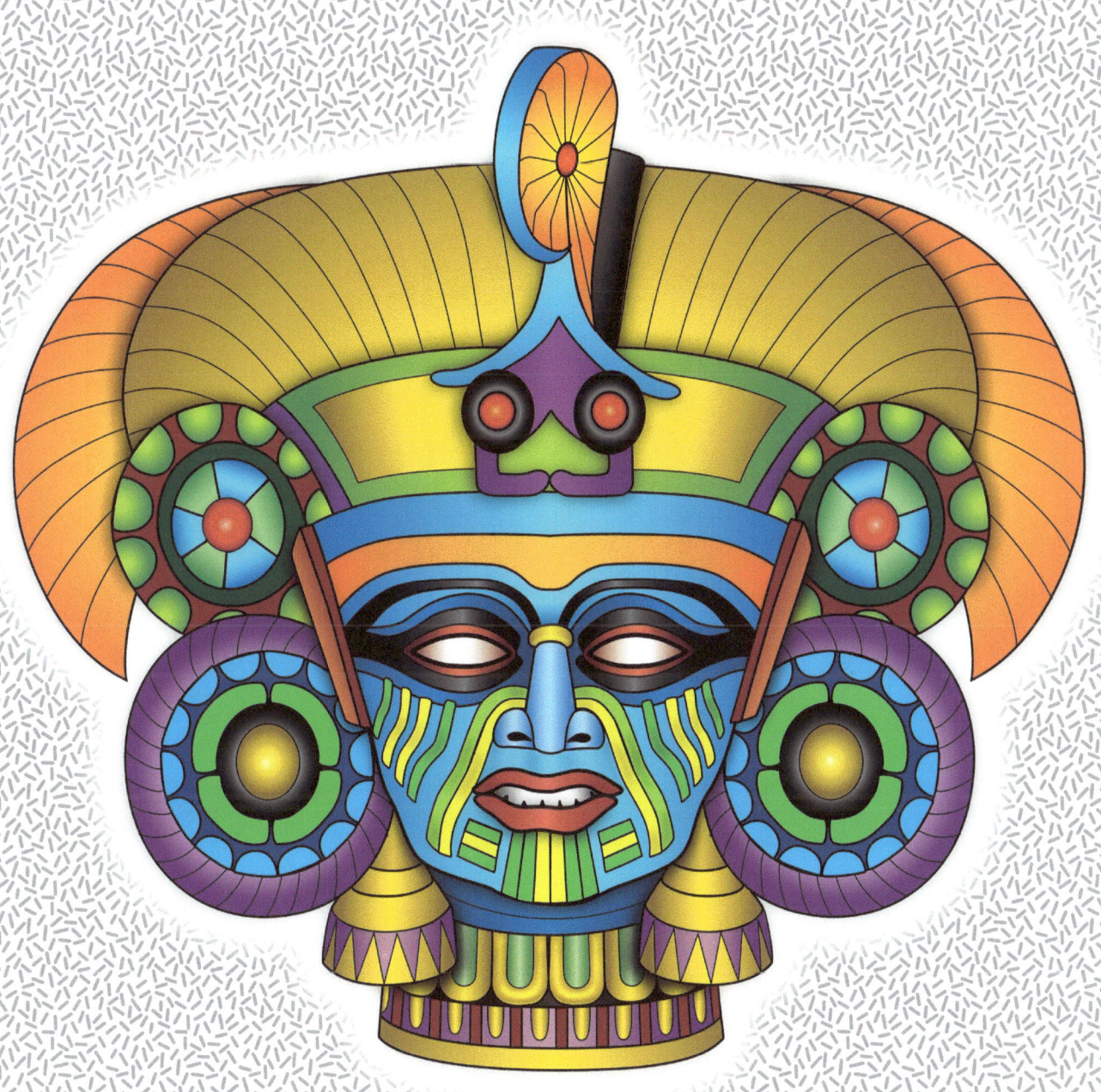

Quetzalpapalotl, the Quetzal-butterfly Aztec god, decorated top and bottom with tributes of the deity. The plume protruding from the headdress is a stylized butterfly proboscis.

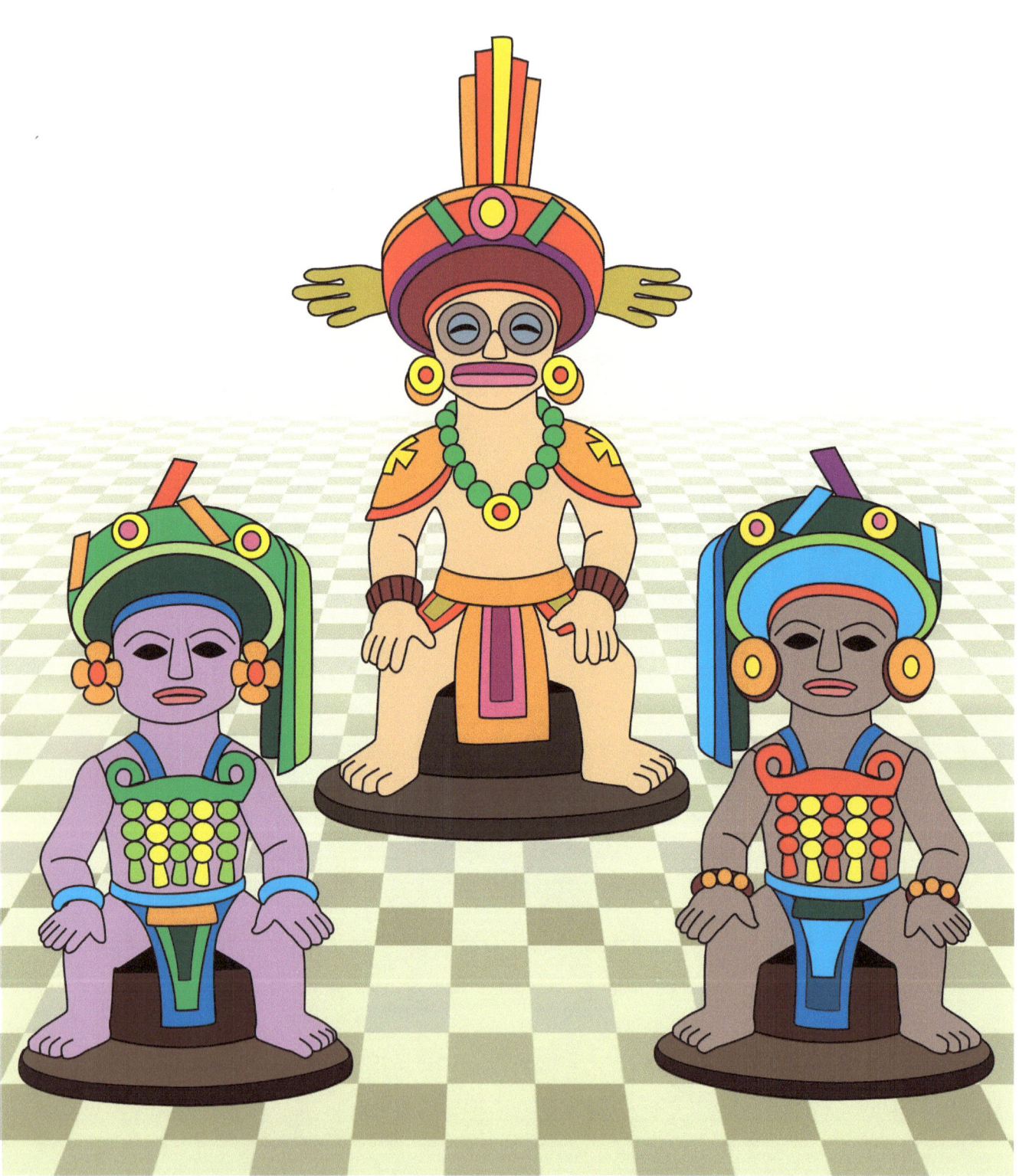

Terracotta figurines found in the city of Copan, ancient Mayan Civilization, Mexico. Possibly figurines are of the Copan rulers.

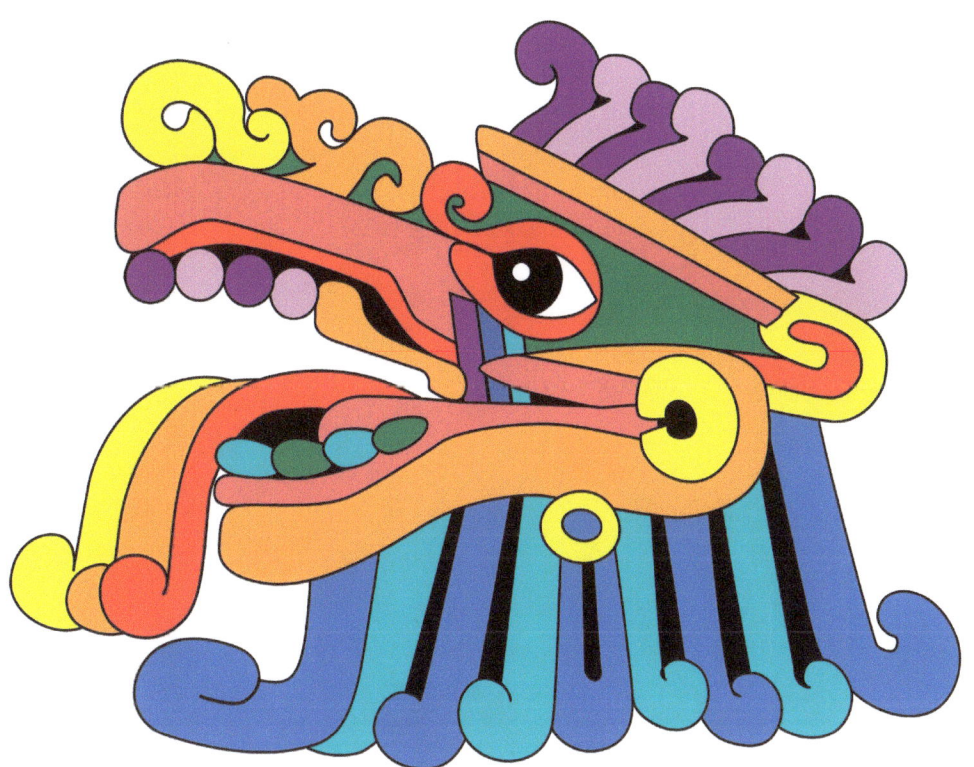

Open fanged head of a feathered serpent worshiped at Xochicalco.

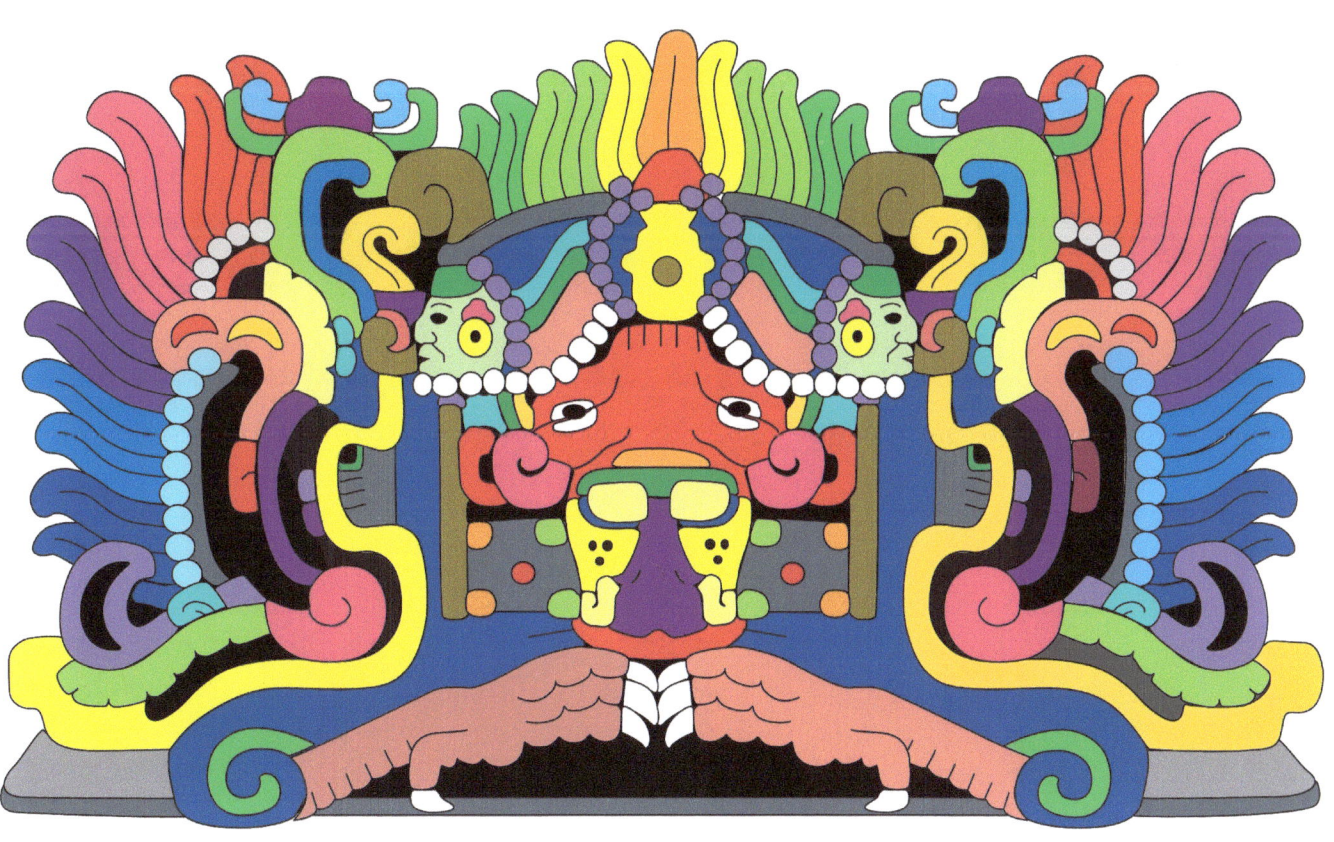

Mayan Stela. Such ornate designs are characteristic of early Mayan art from 300 - 600 C.E.

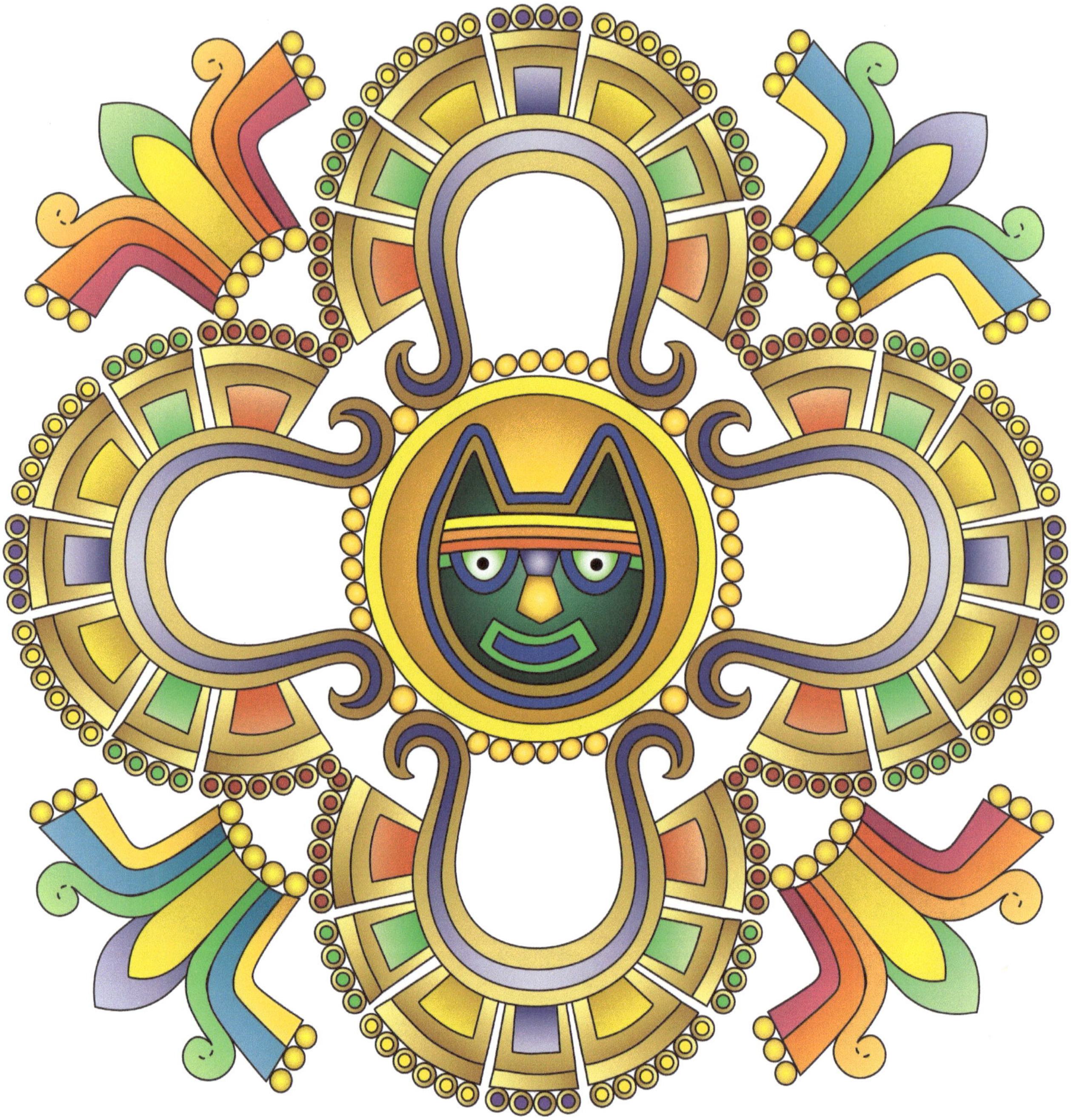

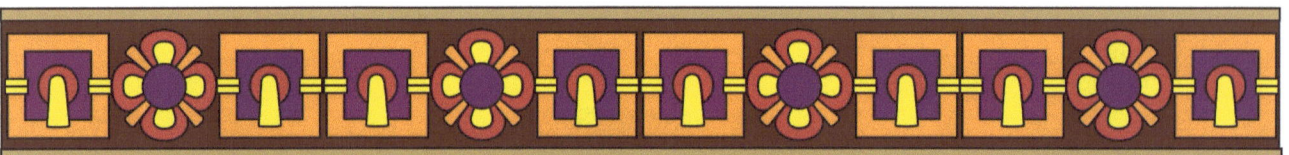

Examples of the images created using the elements found in Pre-Columbian Art.

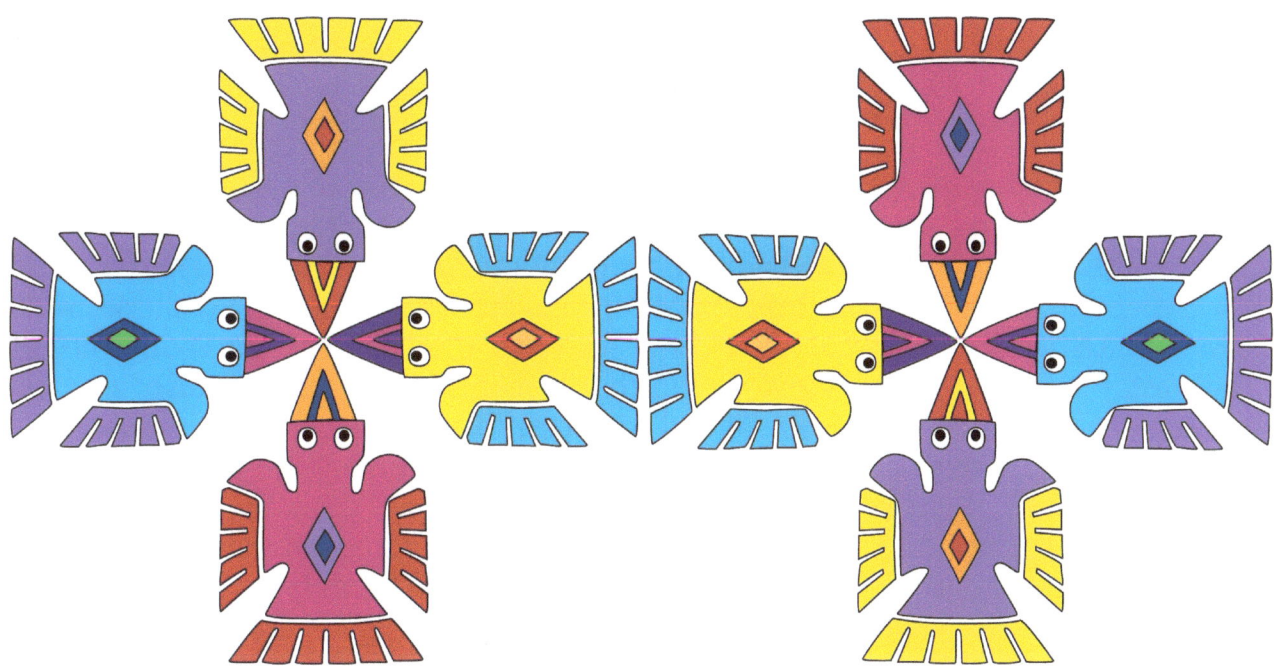

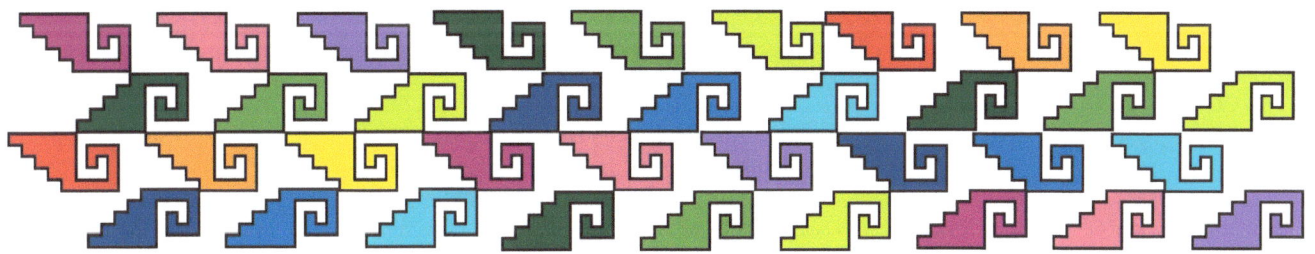

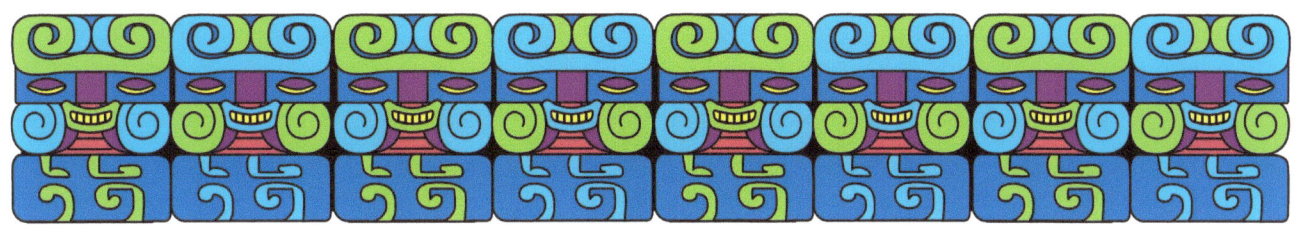

Examples of the images created using the elements found in Pre-Columbian Art.

= a synopsis of =

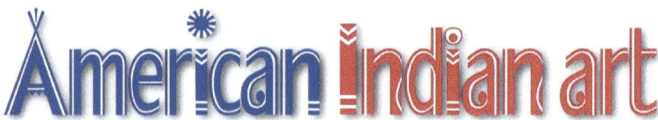
American Indian art

Indigenous Art or more commonly known as North American Indian Art is astonishingly diverse containing forms of art, created by the original inhabitants of North America and their cognate descendants. It carries several different cultures within the category and spans a great time sequence ranging from prehistoric era to present time. North American First Nations art has been divided into five major regions of the continent: The South, The East, The West, The Northwest Coast, and The North. The role of the artists has been to arouse an emotional response from the audience. Their art encompassed the sacred, the secular, ceremonial, commercial, political, and even the domestic.

The surviving artifacts demonstrate that the ancient man had a considerable amount of aesthetic ability. The artists skillfully produced well-balanced forms in both pottery and stone carvings alike. Originally color was achieved from mineral pigments and vegetable dyes and later supplemented by commercial dyes and trade colors.

The Native tradition did not necessarily establish an object's relative value with its purely material and visual features. The visual pleasure from a Cree woman's bitten birch-bark, a pattern is the reality of her inner vision. In the North, Yupik artists depicted mystical journeys of Shamans in carved and painted masks. In the Northwest Coast, masks were exhibited in potlatches which represented the wearer's inherited powers and prerogatives about the location of the political power. Iroquois, in the Northwest, are famous for making False Face Society masks, Quillwork, Beadwork, and Wooden bowls. The Haidas brilliantly crafted the Crest and Totem poles as memorials, that can reach a height of 60 feet or more.

While men's art were mainly representational, women's art were more commonly abstract. Men traditionally carved ritual pipes and masks, and women created artwork associated with clay, fiber, and basketry. The Pueblo women in the New Mexico region have crafted outstanding baskets and pottery.

New York Abstract Expressionists like Jackson Pollock (1912-1956), Barnett Newman (1905-1970), and the Canadian Group of Seven members have grounded their art in the traditional indigenous art of North America.

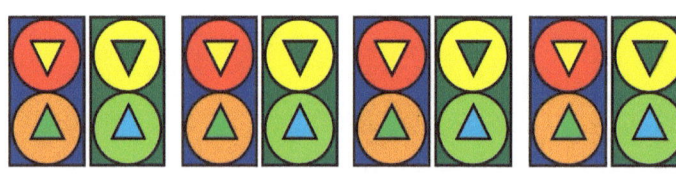

= a synopsis of =

Pre-Columbian Art

The Pre-Columbian Civilization evolved in America in total isolation. It began in 2500 B.C.E., and survived till 1500 C.E., and includes Mayan, Aztec, and Inca Civilizations.

Mayan art is considered to be one of the most beautiful and sophisticated arts of the ancient Western hemisphere. The Mayan Civilization began to flourish in Peten around 1000 B.C.E. It experienced the most development from 200 B.C.E. to 700 C.E., as early classic period, and from 700 C.E. till 10th Century C.E., as the late classic period. Mayan relics can be found scattered throughout Mexico, Guatemala, Honduras, Belize and El Salvador.

During this period, Mayan pottery, sculpture, and writings bloomed as well. Mayans achieved in the arts and their science surpassed all other Pre-Columbian cultures. Mayan writings have been preserved on stone stelae, molded stucco relief embellishments, wooden doors, ceramic vessels and jade ornaments. Mayan hieroglyphic writing comprised of 800 - 1000 symbols, out of which about 200 have been deciphered.

Pre-Columbian Mesoamerican calendar was composed of eighteen months. Each day had a name and they were represented by a unique symbol. Mayan sculptures were masterpieces that were carved out of different materials like, stone, wood, and jade. Mayan paintings inside the caves and temples depicted scenes of mythology, battles, and sacrifice through vivid colors. The Olmecs, founders of Mesoamerica's first civilization, were also Mexico's first sculptors. Using simple tools, they carved volcanic basalt into huge monuments, including colossal portrait heads and alters, and turned the stone into highly polished work of art.

Aztec people were composed of seven tribes. The predatory Aztec tribe left the legendary city of Chicomoztoc and settled on an island in Lake Texcoco, a site in modern Mexico city. Tenochtitlan was the capital of the Aztecs, and was founded in 1325 C.E. The most intricately carved Aztec relic is the circular stone called, The Calendar Stone. The glyphs and the icons adorned it were a road map of the Aztecs destiny. It was discovered in 1790 C.E., beneath Mexico City's central square. Aztec pyramids were known as houses of the Gods and the twin temples dedicated to two gods.

Like the Aztecs, the Incas developed the last empire in Peru at about 1000 C.E. The Incas were the natives of the region extending from Lake Titicaca to Huaraz, settled in the Curico valley where they found their capital. The Inca states extended their empire from Ecuador in the North all the way to Chile in the South.

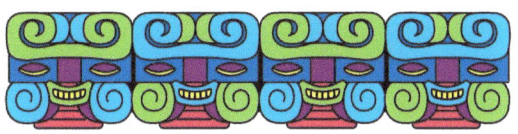

On a decorated stone vessel. Ulua Valley.

OTHER TITLES IN THIS SERIES

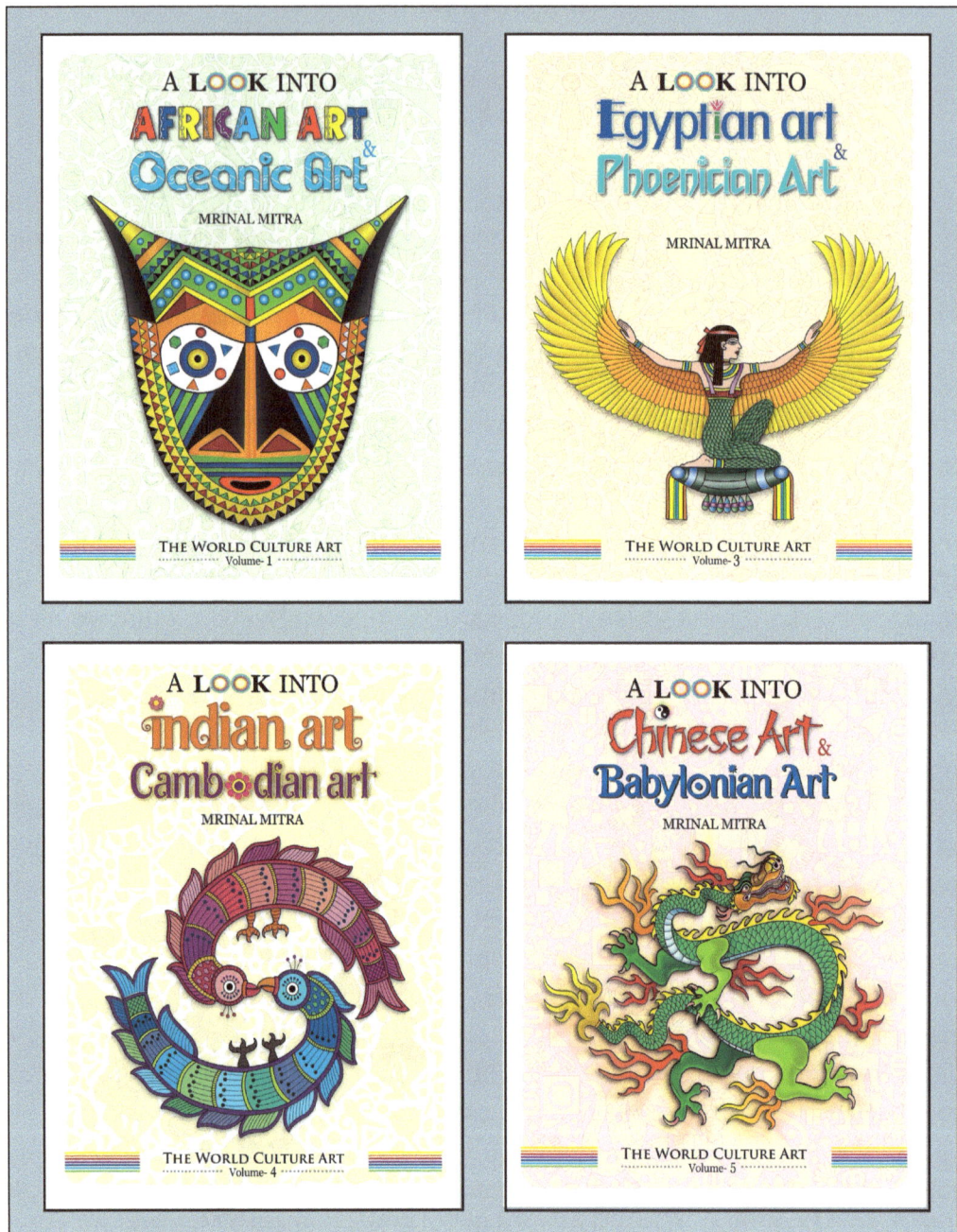

About the Author

Mrinal Mitra has earned a number of prestigious awards, both Indian and International, and received honors for his outstanding illustrations. Some of his recognitions include; The Noma Concours Award (twice), Tokyo, Japan, Illustrators Award, and Children's Choice Award, India, and Honors from German Television `Transtel`, BRNO- CSSR, TIBI- Iran, and UNICEF, New York, USA.

Many of his talented artworks have been exhibited in various countries such as; India, Japan, Italy, Czech Republic, Iran, and New Zealand. Mitra has authored, designed, and illustrated trades and educational children books for many Indian as well as Multinational Book Publishers around the globe.

Printed by CreateSpace, an Amazom.com company.
Available from Amazon.com, CreateSpace.com, and other retail outlets.